WITH G-D AT MY SIDE

A Child's Story of Survival

*Menachem Taiblum
with Cyndie Meyer*

Copyright © 2014 Menachem Taiblum
All rights reserved.

ISBN: 1505862272
ISBN 13: 9781505862270
Library of Congress Control Number: 2014922954
CreateSpace Independent Publishing Platform
North Charleston, South Carolina

DEDICATION

This book was written with tears and prayers.
It is dedicated to my family who were murdered by the Nazis.

Thank you.
G-D Bless you.

Haiblum

PSALM 118:6-9, 17

The Lord is on my side; I will not fear. What can man do to me?
The Lord is my helper; I shall look in triumph on those who hate me.
It is better to take refuge in the Lord than to trust in man.
It is better to take refuge in the Lord than to trust in princes.

I shall not die, but live, and exalt the name of the Lord.

ACKNOWLEDGEMENTS

I started writing this book in my teen years in my mother tongue, Yiddish. I knew Polish of course. Over the years I learned a little Russian and a little Italian. In Israel I spoke and wrote in Hebrew. I wrote some of this there. When I went to work in Brazil, of course I learned Portuguese. I wrote more there. After moving to America, English became my seventh language. By this time I realized the book needed to be written in English. I had to start all over again. I would need help. Once more my help came from G-d.

I wish to acknowledge and thank Jane Schindler for her help with spelling and English grammar and her loving Jewish mothers guilt, which kept me focused on my job of writing.

I wish to give my deepest thanks to Cyndie Meyers, my friend, editor and co-translator without whose hundreds of hours of research and devotion to the project, this book would not have gotten done. I also want to thank her husband Gene, and her two daughters for allowing her to share so much time helping me.

Then there are my friends Sheldon Klapper and Sue Hickey. They deserve my deepest gratitude and thanks for making the great effort to get this story published in the way that would reach the most people with my message – Remember, Remember, Remember!

Mignonne Aquino, my assistant who is my computer person gets all my appreciation for her dedication and help. Every family has a grandson who teaches the older generation about computers, and I am thankful to be able to borrow Mignonne's son Cesar for that purpose. As my tech support he has been very knowledgeable and helpful.

I would like to express my gratitude, to my friend Marinel Mikeja, for bringing all his equipment to take my portrait and for many other pictures. I wish him good luck in all his endeavors.

There are so many friends that I cannot even remember all their names, who encouraged and helped me get my story written and my book published. I want you all to know I appreciate your help, and I thank you very much. May G-d bless you all.

PREFACE

I remember a time before the war, before Nazis invaded Poland, before the bombing, before the holocaust, before the murder of six million Jews. I remember when Jews and Poles lived together in relative peace, and neighbors experienced the joys and trials of life side-by-side, regardless of religious beliefs. My memories of childhood are filled with warmth and love, with friends and family, with learning, praying, and playing.

In those days of innocence, I never anticipated that my childhood would take such a turn and end so differently.

TABLE OF CONTENTS

ACKNOWLEDGEMENTS		vii
PREFACE		ix
CHAPTER 1	A STUBBORN CHILD	1
CHAPTER 2	GROWING UP IN WARSAW	4
CHAPTER 3	ANTI-SEMITISM GROWS IN POLAND	9
CHAPTER 4	NAZIS CONTROL WARSAW	14
CHAPTER 5	THROUGH THE GHETTO WALL FOR FOOD	22
CHAPTER 6	"THE NAZIS CAME AND TOOK EVERYONE AWAY"	27
CHAPTER 7	"IT ISN'T SAFE TO BE JEWISH HERE NOW"	31
CHAPTER 8	HOPPING A TRAIN	36
CHAPTER 9	WORKING FOR FOOD AND SHELTER	41
CHAPTER 10	"ANYONE WITH NO BIRTH CERTIFICATE IS A JEW"	46

CHAPTER 11	"THIS IS YOUR NEW NAME – MARIAN REDLICKI"	50
CHAPTER 12	WORK FOR FOOD, AND MASS EVERY SUNDAY	54
CHAPTER 13	HARD WORK AND A STUBBORN HORSE	58
CHAPTER 14	VOLUNTEERING TO BUILD A BRIDGE	62
CHAPTER 15	THIS IS A LABOR CAMP. YOU WORK FOR THE REICH.	66
CHAPTER 16	A BOY NAMED OLEK – AND OUR ESCAPE	71
CHAPTER 17	HEADED TO WARSAW	77
CHAPTER 18	WE ARE HERE BECAUSE WE WANT TO FIGHT	81
CHAPTER 19	JEWS ARE SHOOTING US	86
CHAPTER 20	WORKING OUR WAY TO THE PARTISANS	89
CHAPTER 21	HE IS JEWISH. WE HAVE TO HELP HIM.	94
CHAPTER 22	DO EITHER OF YOU BOYS KNOW HOW TO USE A GUN?	99
CHAPTER 23	LOSING A FINGER IN A NAZI RAID	103
CHAPTER 24	THE WAR IS OVER!	108
CHAPTER 25	A SENSE OF PREDICTIBILITY AND NORMALCY	115
CHAPTER 26	RETRACING STEPS BACK TO WARSAW	122
CHAPTER 27	SEARCHING THE LISTS OF SURVIVORS	130
CHAPTER 28	MEETING A MESSENGER FROM ISRAEL	137
POST SCRIPT		149

CHAPTER 1
A STUBBORN CHILD

"Menachem! You must come in now," my father's voice echoed off the apartment buildings and shops that lined Panska Street. It was a warm afternoon in 1938. I was nine years old, and my friends and I chased each other up and down the cobbled Warsaw avenue, ducking past carts and wagons, horses, and pedestrians.

I looked over my shoulder. Father waited in the doorway of his shop, his grocer's apron tied around his middle. "Menachem!" he called again. "Do you hear me? It is time to come in. I need your help!"

One of my chums ran beside me, his cheeks glowing with youth and vigor. "Race you to the end of the block," he said.

I glanced at my father again. "I'll be there in a minute, Father," I shouted, waving.

"No, Menachem! You must come now!" Father yelled in Yiddish, his full red beard and long curly sideburns bouncing up and down.

I turned my back on him and raced after my friend. I knew what Father wanted: every Friday I collected payments from customers who bought groceries "on the book." It was time to get started, but today I was determined to enjoy every possible second of sunshine and fun.

I glanced over my shoulder as I ran. Father still stood in the doorway, frowning, his hands on his hips. Customers lined up behind him, waiting to buy last-minute items before Shabbat began at sunset. Father had work to do, and I was pushing the limits of his patience.

I ran with all my might to the end of the block.

"I win!" I shouted, feeling victorious at being the first to reach the goal. I patted my friend on the back. "I've got to get home now. My father needs me."

I waved at my father again. I was satisfied with the fun I'd had.

"C'mon. Just one more race," my friend answered.

"No, I really have to go. Maybe we can play again on Sunday."

As I approached the shop, I heard Father admonish me: "It's late, son. Hurry, so you get back before we light the Shabbos candles."

I was steps from the store when my friend grabbed my cap and ran off, laughing.

"Hey!" I shouted. The warm spring air ruffled my brown hair and the excitement of the chase made my heart skip a beat. I whirled around, forgetting about Father. I took the first step to chase after my friend, when I felt something pinch my ear.

"Ouch!" I yelped.

I looked up. Father's hand was a vice on my ear. His face was as red as the tomatoes in his store, and beads of sweat popped on his forehead.

"Ouch, let go!" I cried. The heat of embarrassment flooded my face and neck as Father twisted my ear and led me past my friends. We marched past waiting customers and through the back door that led to our apartment. There, Father gave me a spanking I still remember.

"Menachem," he declared, "you are a stubborn child."

"Yes, Father," I whimpered.

"You must control your strong will, or it will cost you dearly throughout your life," he predicted.

I never forgot that afternoon. I never forgot my father's disappointment or the lessons he tried to teach me that day, and every day, of my young life.

In many ways, my father was right: My strong will would cost me dearly in the years ahead, but it also served me well. In fact, my stubborn streak would save my life: I would survive the horrors yet to come, often because I was simply too stubborn to give up—and because G-d was at my side.

CHAPTER 2
GROWING UP IN WARSAW

I grew up in the Jewish Quarter of Warsaw, Poland, the eldest of the three children. Our family lived in the two-bedroom apartment my mother had lived in as a child. More than 100 of our relatives lived within walking distance of our home, and my brother, Yosef, our little sister, Chana, and I never lacked attention or a cousin with whom to play. Our family had lived in Warsaw for generations, and we considered ourselves as Polish as anyone in the city.

My mother, Rosa, was a meticulous housekeeper, and ours was a cozy home. A door at the rear of our apartment connected to my father's grocery store, which opened onto Panska Street. From morning to night, my father, Israel, bustled around his shop, welcoming customers and straightening merchandise.

My parents were orthodox Jews who belonged to the pious Hasidic branch of our religion. My father, like all Hasidic men, always wore a white dress shirt and black trousers. A white prayer shawl called a *tallit*, wrapped over his shoulders, and his head was always covered out of respect for G-d who is above. When indoors, he wore a small round cap called a *yarmulke*. When he went outdoors, he wore a silk fedora.

Hasidic men never cut their facial hair, so my father had a full red beard that reached his chest, and long sideburns, called forelocks, that curled in front of his ears.

Mother was taller and sturdier than Father. Like all Hasidic women, she was very modest and covered her hair with a kerchief or wig. She had large brown eyes that twinkled when she laughed. She was a strong, kind woman and a loving, caring mother.

My family's religious faith shaped and guided our lives. We measured the passing of each day with prayers, and each year was punctuated with religious holidays. Every morning at sunrise, Father and I walked several blocks to pray at our small neighborhood temple or *shul*. Our prayers continued throughout the day, before and after meals, in the evening, and before we went to bed.

The week began at sunset on Friday when Mother lit the *Shabbos* (Sabbath) candles and recited prayers to welcome a new week. She prepared her most delicious recipes and served them on special china and silver that had been treasured in our family for generations. On Saturday mornings, we dressed in our best clothes and walked to *shul*, then spent the afternoon resting and visiting with relatives.

On holidays, we observed centuries-old traditions, and my relatives gathered to eat and celebrate together. Every autumn, we celebrated *Sukkot* by building an outdoor shelter called a *Sukkah* in the courtyard of my aunt's apartment building. For eight days and nights, my family ate all of our meals there with our relatives and thanked G-d for the harvest, nature, and all our blessings.

We were eating dinner in the *Sukkah* one evening when my father caught me holding my spoon in my left hand. In our culture, the left hand was considered "dirty" and was never to be used for eating. Yet, here I was, handling food with my "dirty" hand in front of our relatives! Father was horrified. This was not the first time I had been warned; after all, I was naturally left-handed. Not wanting to attract our relative's attention, Father tapped my shin under the table with his foot. I immediately switched the spoon to my right hand, and I never ate or wrote with my left hand again.

Of all holidays, my favorite was Chanukah, when we celebrated a rededication of the temple in Jerusalem that had occurred almost 2000 years before. On each of eight dark, wintery nights, we lit an extra candle on our *menorah* until, on the last night, it blazed like a bonfire with the light of all nine candles. We sang songs and exchanged small gifts such as prayer books and games.

Father saw the holidays as a special opportunity for generosity. At Chanukah, he made sure even the poorest child in the Jewish Quarter received a gift. Again in the spring, he delivered boxes of food to poor families before Passover. He included traditional items, like salt, matzah, bitter herbs, and a lamb bone, so they could have a proper Seder dinner.

My father had a reputation as a generous and dependable man. Both he and Mother were living examples of the lesson they taught us every day of their lives: Love your neighbor as yourself.

One chilly morning, we hurried to the shop after *shul*, when a funeral procession for someone we didn't know came down the street.

"Wait, Menachem," Father commanded. He took my hand, and we watched respectfully as a horse-drawn hearse slowly made its way down the street. Following behind it came a handful of elderly women, dressed in black.

I noticed Father counting the mourners. "Oh, no!" he gasped, "there aren't enough men for a respectable burial." According to Jewish tradition, a *Minyan*—10 men over the age of 13—was required to recite *Kaddish*, the prayer for the dead, at the cemetery. If there were not enough men, Jewish tradition said the prayers might go unheard. Father counted again, then shook his head.

"Menachem, I must go to the cemetery. You know the way home. Just stay to our usual route, and I will be there soon," he said. He did not hesitate a second before joining the procession.

My father was compulsive about opening his shop on time, because farmers came early to drop off their goods. I had never seen him open the store late, but to him, this was a greater need. Father didn't know the man who died, or anyone else in the funeral party, yet he walked and prayed with the mourners as if he had planned it all along. Later, he told me the greatest thing he could do for another person was an act of kindness for which they were unable to say "thank you."

My father and mother taught me another lesson: to judge no one. One day, on the way home from *shul*, my father and I passed a beggar. The old man leaned against a building, his hand outstretched. Father took coins from his pocket and handed them to the man. An acquaintance of Father's saw this and said, "Israel, why are you giving money to this man? He has money. He doesn't need to beg."

Father thought for a few seconds, then answered, "My friend, who are we to judge? If this man takes money from someone who needs it, he will be judged by a higher authority, but not by me."

This was not the only occasion when my father's actions impressed me. He was always kind and thought more about others than he did about himself. He visited the sick and was one of the only people in our community allowed to prepare people's bodies for burial.

Father's reputation as a fair and honest businessman made his store successful, and it overflowed with customers. I often lingered to watch him work and to listen to the adults' conversations. I once overheard a customer ask why my father's store was always full when, only a block away, another store was always empty.

My father shrugged and answered with a grin: "Perhaps because I am happy to make less profit and sell more, and the other grocer wants to sell less and make more."

Father loaded his store's shelves with sacks of flour, rice, and beans. Every day, local farmers pulled horse-drawn wagons to the curb and delivered fresh milk, butter, eggs, and cheese right through the front door. They replenished the barrels and baskets of potatoes, onions, beets, turnips, and carrots that lined the walls.

One of the farmers who sold vegetables to our store came from the nearby village of Tarczyn. He and Father became good friends, and when I was seven years old, father let me spend the day at his farm. On the way there, I sat in the front of the wagon, next to the farmer, noticing every turn in the road and every landmark along the way. I marveled at the open green fields and sweet, fresh air. When we got to the farm, I played with baby lambs and chicks and pulled radishes and onions straight from the ground. It was a memorable break from the crowded, gray streets of Warsaw.

Like most Polish Jews, my family spoke Yiddish at home and prayed in Hebrew. When I was three, I began to attend *cheder,* a Hebrew school where children learned to say their prayers. By the age of five, I was learning to read and write in Yiddish, and when I was seven, I started public school and studied Polish. My brother and sister also attended school. We studied and played with both Jewish and non-Jewish children from our neighborhood. My classmates were my best friends, and I never expected that to change.

CHAPTER 3
ANTI-SEMITISM GROWS IN POLAND

My family was happy, comfortable and well fed until I was around six years old. In 1935, things began to change.

One afternoon, I found my father standing in a corner of his grocery store, crying. "Father, what has happened?" I asked, feeling alarmed.

"*Zaide* passed away," he said. *Zaide* is Yiddish for "grandfather," and I immediately began to sob, wondering which of my two grandfathers had died.

"Which *Zaide*?" I whimpered.

Seeing my tears, Father put his arm around me and explained: "No, Menachem. Not our *Zaide*. I am talking about *Zaide* Pilsudski, Poland's president. Pilsudski was so good to us Jews, that we called him 'grandfather'."

We closed the store early that day, and took a trolley to Pilsudski's home at Belvedere Palace. We joined a long line of mourners that wrapped around the building and waited patiently to pay respect to the man lying in the casket. When our turn came, I peered at the big, handsome man. I thought he looked as if he were alive.

Pilsudski had always been a hero to Poland's Jews. Until the day Pilsudski died, Jewish life in Poland was not so bad, but the following day, Edward Rydz-Smigly took office. He gave anti-Semites a free hand, and feelings that had been buried for years were suddenly exposed. Immediately, Jewish life in Poland took a turn for the worse. Anti-Semitic signs, profanity, and graffiti appeared on buildings across Poland. It seemed that everywhere we turned, we read: "Don't buy from Jews!" "Send Jews to Palestine!" "Death to Jews!"

Jewish men—especially orthodox Jews who were easily identified by their appearance—became targets for abuse. Our tormentors tore the traditional clothing of Jewish men and cut and ripped the beards and forelocks from their faces. Young hoodlums preyed on Jewish children and the elderly, beating and bullying them. We were publicly humiliated, embarrassed, and degraded.

At school and in my neighborhood, most of the children were not Jewish. After Pilsudski died, my non-Jewish friends acted as if they didn't know me anymore. They called me a "dirty Jew." When they saw me, they turned their backs and ran away. I was excluded from their games, their conversations, and their studies.

I was confused and hurt. I felt lonely and heartbroken. These children had been my friends for as long as I could remember. Our families had lived next door to each other for years. My father did business with their parents. Now, they taunted and laughed at my family and me. Everything changed so quickly, and I could not understand why.

Father was right about the history of Poland. King Casimir the Great invited Europe's Jews to move to Poland in the 1300s. He created laws to protect us, and for hundreds of years after that, Poland welcomed Jews who migrated from less tolerant countries such as Spain and Germany. Over time, Poland became the center of Jewish culture in Europe. By 1931, more than 3 million Jews lived in Poland—375,000 in Warsaw—almost a third of Warsaw's total population.

Although we considered Poland our home, the Polish people began to resent us. They grew suspicious of our religious dress and customs. By the 1930s, more and more Jewish refugees came to Poland from other countries, and resentment grew into outright violence and hatred.

In 1937, a man named Ze'ev Jabotinsky, visited Warsaw. He came from Israel, which was then called Palestine, and he gave a famous speech about the impending threat to Jews in Europe. Jabotinsky warned that a black cloud of danger and anti-Semitism was gathering in Europe. He said it would eventually wipe out all Jews who lived there. "Save yourselves while there is still time," he begged. He urged us to leave Europe and move to Palestine. He predicted Israel would someday be an independent country, a homeland for Jews.

Although most Jews thought Jabotinsky was crazy and didn't take him seriously, some Jews listened and moved to Palestine, the United States, or South America. Father was not one of them. He remained in Warsaw and hoped for better days. Like so many others, he never believed humans could be capable of the evil that was yet to come.

My father and I attended Jabotinski's speech along with hundreds of other Jews. When it was over, the sidewalks and streets near the auditorium bulged with people discussing his message. Father joined them, eager to exchange opinions with relatives and friends.

I was soon bored of all of the talk. I looked around for a distraction and immediately found one: a Gypsy band arrived to play music and pass the hat. I always loved the Gypsies' Roma music, so I left Father's side and wandered closer.

The rich sound of the violin, tambourine, and concertina enveloped me. I inched closer for a better view and became totally absorbed in their performance. When the crowd outside the auditorium dispersed, the musicians moved on, playing and singing. I followed them from street to street and soon lost track of how much time had passed and how far I had wandered.

Eventually, the crowd dwindled as people went home for dinner. Without warning, the Gypsies suddenly packed their instruments, hopped on a trolley, and disappeared. I found myself standing on an unfamiliar street corner—alone, frightened, and lost. I had no idea where I was, or how to get home.

I began to wail. Tears rolled down my cheeks. Would I ever get home? Where was Mama? Where was Father?

I remained glued to the street corner, crying loudly, until a policeman walked by. "What's the matter, little fella?" he asked.

"I'm lost and I don't know how to find my way home," I mumbled.

"Do you know your address?" he asked.

"Yes. I live at No. 59 Panska Street, but I don't know how to get there." I wiped my eyes on my sleeve and looked up at him hopefully.

"My goodness! That is a long way from here. What happened?" he asked.

I told the policeman that I had followed the beautiful music, but the musicians left suddenly. He listened and I talked, and we began to walk down the street together. I reached out and took his hand. It felt enormous, but safe, as it closed around my tiny fingers. The policeman was gentle and kind. He walked me all the way home and delivered me to my doorstep. My mother met us at the door and thanked the policeman over and over again.

My father and his friends were searching our district, asking if anyone had seen me. When he returned home, Father was overjoyed to find I was safe and unharmed. He said I had already suffered enough for one day and didn't punish me for causing so much worry.

Over the next few years, circumstances grew more and more difficult for Polish Jews, and some decided to leave the country. My aunt moved to Argentina. She wrote to my father and begged him to sell his store and join her, but he refused. He said Jews had lived in Poland for more than 600 years, and he would not be among the first to leave.

"This is my home," he wrote to his sister. "My great grandparents, grandparents, parents, and children were born here—and we will die here." His statement was prophetic, sooner than he expected. The rest of my family were all murdered by the Nazis.

CHAPTER 4
NAZIS CONTROL WARSAW

Over the next months, we began to see the truth in Jabotinski's message. Day after day, life grew more difficult for the Jews of Poland, but by then, it was too late. Less than a year after Jabotinski's speech, Nazis invaded our country.

In the days before the invasion, most people turned to their radios for the latest news. My father didn't think radios were part of G-d's plan. Instead, he followed the Nazi's progress through Europe by reading one of several Yiddish newspapers published in Warsaw. Every afternoon, he sent me down the street with a few coins to buy his paper, then he scoured it for news. That's how we knew when the Nazis were getting closer, but nothing prepared us for the invasion on September 1, 1939.

Within a week after the Nazis crossed Poland's border, the sound of air raid sirens wailed through Warsaw. Fighter planes buzzed overhead. The Nazis knew their targets, and bombs dropped in the south and west parts of the city. As the days went on, bombing intensified, and the city filled with smoke and fire. My family had nowhere to hide, so we huddled in our apartment and prayed. The worst bombing took place on Yom Kippur, one of the holiest days of the Jewish year.

By the end of September, the Polish army surrendered, and Nazis controlled Warsaw. They immediately enforced new restrictions and imposed laws targeting Jews. They required Jews over the age of 12 to wear armbands clearly marked with the Star of David. We were not allowed to walk on the sidewalk with non-Jews. We could not ride the regular streetcar. Food was rationed, and Jews were given a smaller allowance than non-Jews. Because we still had our store, my family was lucky: we ate the food we had planned to sell.

The Nazis banned Jews from working in many professions. They froze our bank accounts and imposed a curfew on Jewish businesses. Father had to close his store by 5 p.m., which was a hardship for him and for customers who worked late. One policeman who always shopped at our store when he finished work at 10 p.m. asked Father to help him. Father decided to ignore the curfew for this man—and for others who needed to feed their families.

To avoid detection, Father told these customers to come to the door of our apartment, which opened to the street behind our store. Father led them through the connecting door into the store and let them gather what they needed. This income helped our family to survive, and the people Father helped were always thankful for the risk my father took to help them. Although we did not know it then, my father's small act of kindness would someday save my life.

In October 1940, the Nazis decreed that Jews could no longer operate businesses or live outside the Jewish Quarter. We were required to move. Our family lived on the outer edge of the Quarter, so my parents thought we were protected and could stay where we were. They were wrong.

One morning, my father answered a loud knock on the door. A wall of blue uniforms filled our doorway. Armed members of the Nazi's Blue Police proclaimed that a new apartment had been "prepared" for us, closer to the center of the Jewish Quarter. We could take only what we could pack in one hour.

Mother and Father looked at each other in disbelief. How could this be happening? Stunned and disheartened, we scrambled through the apartment, packing what we could into bundles and boxes. Mother grabbed the silverware, the silver Passover candlesticks, and anything of value. Father packed food from the store, and Mother dressed us children in as many layers of clothing as we could wear.

Everything was chaos. How could we pack an entire lifetime in a single hour? How could we choose what to take? It was impossible; so we packed what we could carry and left everything else behind.

Once outside, we joined a few other Jewish families who were also forced from their homes and businesses on Panska Street. Chana held Mother's hand as we followed the policemen up the road. "Mama, where are we going? Father, why are we going?" my sister asked over and over. Mother didn't answer, but tears rolled down her cheeks. Father never said a word.

Urged on by the police, Mother turned her back on the only home she had ever known. She abandoned all the possessions her family had treasured. Father walked away from his store, his investment, and his livelihood.

I looked up at the tall apartment buildings that loomed over Panska Street. A few familiar faces peered from the windows, but most of our neighbors were hiding, afraid to be seen. They knew they could not save us and feared that any sign of friendship could cause trouble. Many were simply glad to see us go.

Along the way, we noticed a tall brick wall, topped with shards of glass and barbed wire. The Nazis had constructed the wall in a matter of weeks to enclose an area slightly larger than a single square mile. This area became known as the Warsaw Ghetto, but the Germans preferred to call it the "Jewish Quarter." Signs at the gate said that a quarantine was in effect, and no one could enter or exit through the gates without permission. To be sure we remained within the walls, guards stood at the gates that separated the Ghetto from the rest of the world. Over the next few years, the Nazis concentrated more than

450,000 Jews from all over Poland and a few neighboring countries into this enclosure.

My family carried our belongings to a second-floor apartment at No. 6 Twarda Street. We pushed the door open and stared into the cramped, dark quarters where five of us would live for the next two years. In the tiny kitchen, a gray streak of sunlight filtered through a lonely, bare window too high for a view. A single, stark light bulb hung from a thick wire in the center of the room. A worn table and two dingy wooden chairs stood next to a coal stove and a cracked, filthy sink.

In the apartment's single bedroom, three straw mattresses slouched on the floor. Every night, I tugged a mattress into the kitchen, while in the bedroom, my father and brother shared another mattress and my sister and mother shared the third.

"We don't want to live here," my brother and I whined. "We want to go home now!" We missed our cozy home, our beds, our books, and the food that was so plentiful in Father's shop. This place was not a home. Home had warm beds, pictures and carpets, beautiful furniture, and toys. This place was cold, dark, frightening, and lonely.

"Hush now," Father whispered. "This is only temporary. It can't last long. We will move home when this insanity is over." Father meant to reassure us, but worry and uncertainty clouded his eyes.

Our apartment was located in a section of the Jewish Quarter known as the Little Ghetto. To the north was the main Ghetto, and a gate at Choldna Street separated the two. Conditions in the Little Ghetto were slightly better than those in the main area. It was a little less crowded, and the buildings weren't as old, but we were still impoverished and desperate. Electricity and clean water were unpredictable luxuries, often halting for hours or days at a time.

Food was rationed, and the amount we were allowed to buy was printed on a ration card. At first, Jews were allowed the same amount as non-Jews, but as weeks went by, Jews were allowed less and less. By 1941, the official ration provided 2613 calories per day for Germans living in Poland, 699 calories for Poles, but only 300 calories for Jews in the Ghetto. Death from starvation and illness was commonplace—especially among the children and elderly. Typhoid fever, dysentery, and tuberculosis were rampant.

The "luckiest" residents of the Ghetto found a way to work, or traded their belongings for money. My father went to work for a bakery. Every morning at sunrise, he strapped a huge basket onto his back, and a baker loaded it with heavy brown loaves of bread. Father was not a tall man, and the basket reached from his shoulders to his knees. He trudged up and down the cobblestone streets of the Ghetto all day, hefting the basket on and off his back, selling and delivering his heavy loaves. It was exhausting work, but Father never complained, and it allowed my family a little extra bread to eat.

I was just a child, but I did what I could to help. Twice each week, I ran to the headquarters of the *kapo*—the Jewish police—and polished the officers' tall, shiny boots. They paid me with scraps of food, which I carried home to share with my family.

The *kapo* were Jews who volunteered to enforce the rules of the Nazis. In return, they were treated better than the rest of us. They claimed to have our best interests in mind, and they insisted our lives would be worse if Germans, Poles, or Ukrainians guarded us. Perhaps this was true, but the *kapo* were not kind people. They were often abusive, and they spied on us and reported everything we said and did to the Nazis. The Nazis told the *kapo* they would be spared because of their service to Hitler's Reich. Of course, this was a lie.

The *kapo* guarded the Ghetto walls and tried to prevent smuggling, but a black market developed nonetheless. Children my age were often the best smugglers. At night, these tiny traders crawled through drainage holes or scaled the Ghetto wall, returning later with food and medicine for their families' use or to sell inside the Ghetto. The black market kept many people alive, but my father said it was too dangerous and forbade me to participate. The law said smugglers could be shot on sight—and that included children. The guards who patrolled the wall had no reservations about enforcing this law. Still, I couldn't help thinking how much I could help my family if I tried.

Instead of smuggling, my mother sent me to the street with our family's best dishes and silver, our family's most treasured belongings. By the age of 11, I was a salesman, standing on the street corner, hawking our valuables. Some Jews who had a lot to sell set up tables on the sidewalks and displayed their wares. I simply carried the items in my hands, walking up and down the street, calling out to passersby. When the Passover candlesticks and silverware were gone, I sold our better pieces of clothing. Poles and Germans entered the Ghetto to purchase our possessions at discounted prices. Some of the wealthier Jews who lived in the Ghetto also bought our belongings, thinking they would enjoy them after the war was over.

I sold our family treasures for far less than they were worth so my family could buy something to eat. Sadly, the available food was barely edible, and I yearned for something tasty and fresh. Mother tried to make our meals as appealing as she could, but no matter how hungry I was, my daily ration of old potatoes seemed disgusting. Finally one evening, I refused to eat the food my mother had scraped together. I shoved my bowl away and ran up five flights of stairs to the top floor of our building. I planned to wait until I was sure Mother had forgotten about me, but I underestimated her. Mother raced after me to the top of the stairs. Panting, she took me by the hand, brought me downstairs, and held me until I finished every bite of that awful meal. She knew that, no matter how distasteful, we had to eat to survive.

During those sad days, I found a source of comfort and inspiration in the synagogue next door. Our apartment building stood next to the historic Nozyk Synagogue where Gerchon Sirota, a world-famous cantor, conducted the choir. I heard the choir when I passed the synagogue one day. I thought it sounded like the singing of angels.

I longed to go inside the synagogue so I could hear them better, but it was a Reform temple, more westernized and liberal than our

Hasidic *shul*. I knew Father would be angry if I entered this non-orthodox building, so I sat outside the window and listened carefully. Eventually, the lure of the music grew too strong. I crept inside and hid between the benches where I could listen without being seen.

Day after day, I returned, hid, and listened while the choir prepared for services. Soon, I knew all of the melodies, and could sing the musical prayers by heart. From my hiding place among the benches, I closed my eyes and hummed along.

I crouched there one afternoon when Sirota himself tapped my shoulder. My eyes flew open, and I found the choirmaster smiling at me.

"*Boychick*," he said, pulling me to my feet, "Why are you hiding? Don't you like the music?"

"Oh yes, very much, sir!"

"Then why don't you sing with us?" he asked. "There is a children's choir for boys your age."

"I don't think my father will let me," I said, quite certain of what my father would say, "but I will ask his permission."

That night, I asked Father if I could sing with the choir next door. My father said nothing, but wagged his finger back and forth to indicate the answer was "no." My father believed, as many orthodox Jews did, that G-d did not hear the prayers of people who were paid to pray. As a paid cantor, Sirota fell into this category.

I was usually an obedient boy, but I decided to disobey my father. I snuck off to the synagogue every chance I got. There, I learned to sing from one of the world's finest vocal artists. Sirota was famous across Europe and America. He had made many records and performed to sold-out audiences at Carnegie Hall in New York City. The American press called him "the Jewish Caruso."

Sirota led the choir with joy and enthusiasm. He taught me to control and project my voice, and although I could never sing with his choir publicly because of my father's rules, I enjoyed the rehearsals immensely.

Sirota and his family survived in Warsaw until the final days of the Ghetto Uprising, but he was ultimately one of 1500 cantors killed during the Holocaust. I fondly remember the gifted man's kindness. His inspiration led me to become a cantor after the war was over.

CHAPTER 5
THROUGH THE GHETTO WALL FOR FOOD

Every afternoon, the men in our neighborhood gathered on the street corners to speculate about what would happen next. My father must have heard about the terrible events in the larger Ghetto, but he protected us from the worst of the news. We continued to hope and pray for the best. Even in the worst of times, we believed our prayers would be answered. Few believed things could get worse.

We were wrong.

On November 16, 1940, the Nazis closed and locked the Ghetto gates. It became illegal for Jews to leave the Ghetto for work, food, or medication. Non-Jews were forbidden to enter. Guards shot anyone who tried to escape.

Years later, I discovered that thousands of Jews were deported to the death camp at Treblinka every single day once the gates were sealed. My parents may have known this, but if they did, they never told us children.

Food became more scarce, and starving people—including children—collapsed and died in the streets of the large Ghetto where my aunt lived. My family stopped visiting and stayed near our apartment in the smaller Ghetto.

It wasn't long before my father lost his job, and we sold the last of our belongings. Without any income, and nothing left to sell, we could not buy food. Many Jews believed the Nazis were starving us to death, while less than a block away, Poles and Germans were relatively well fed.

My family had survived within the Ghetto for nearly two years at this point. Now, we were starving to death. My stomach was always empty, and my sister and brother's skinny arms and legs looked like skeletons. Their eyes were enormous, and they no longer smiled. Father and mother were despondent. I knew we would die if we did not eat; yet there was nothing we could do but pray for a miracle.

I felt frustrated, angry, and powerless. I was now 12 years old, and under better circumstances, I would have been preparing for my *Bar Mitzvah*, the ceremony when Jewish boys are recognized as men. This weighed on my mind, and one night, I dreamed a vivid dream in which I composed a speech for my *Bar Mitzvah* service. I saw myself dressed in a beautiful new prayer shawl. I felt joyful, and I saw pride on my Father's face.

I was awakened when a thin ray of sunlight filtered through our grimy kitchen window. I looked around and realized I was still in the Ghetto. My stomach was empty and my family was still hungry. I would never need a *Bar Mitzvah* speech, because there would never be a *Bar Mitzvah* celebration for me.

Sorrow enveloped me as my beautiful dream evaporated, but it left a profound impact. I realized that I was nearly a man. My family was starving, and I had to do something. Perhaps it was time to sneak through the Ghetto wall to get some food. I knew kids who smuggled. They had shown me a hole through the wall. But, even if I could get through the wall, where would I go for help?

I remembered the farmer who delivered produce to our grocery store before the war—the one who had taken me to his farm for the weekend. He was kind and generous. If I could find a way to get through the wall undetected, perhaps I could find my way there and ask him for help. My heart raced with hope. I convinced myself I could remember how to get to the farm. If I snuck out at night, no one would notice I was gone. Surely the farmer would give me food, and I could race back and surprise my family in the morning.

I imagined returning to the Ghetto, loaded down with bags of food. Like a man, I would save my family. My parents would be proud. My sister and brother's faces would light with joy. Mother would cook a wonderful meal, and we would feast and then sleep with full bellies.

With these ideas spinning in my head, it was impossible to sleep. My stomach growled with hunger, and I shivered in the cold. I found a scrap of paper and a pencil. Then, leaning against the wall, I pulled my thin blanket around me and jotted down the lines of a poem:

"On a still, cold night,
I sit on my little bed
Tired, sick and I think:
Where will I go?
How will I find some bread
So my brother and sister won't die of hunger?
I do not think long,
And as it is still dark
And as it is still night,
I go into the Ghetto
And into the street
To look for some bread and food
For my brother and sister.
I run through the streets
Past burned out houses

And don't encounter a soul.
I walk tirelessly, exhausted,
Past houses, down alleys,
As a lamb to the slaughter.
I go into a house
From which I can
Pass to the other side of the Ghetto.
I barely move in the stillness
With a broken heart and a broken will.
And suddenly,
Not knowing from where,
I hear a wild cry:
"Where are the Juden who are hiding in there?"
Oh poor, poor me.
Now my troubles will end
And I will abandon
This bitter Exile.
Silently I shiver and huddle in the dark.
Not a bark from a dog can be heard.
And when the town clock strikes three
I can say joyously:
"Death did go by.
Now the time has come to move on."
I leave the burned-out houses
And run through the streets
Through the fields, through the woods,
And come to the spot
And take some bread
And with stifled sobs, run home
Where my people wait for me.
And no one will ask where I came from,
Where I have been,
But will fall to eating bread."

When I finished writing, I rolled the paper around my little pencil and tucked it deep into my pocket. I studied the poem many times that day, considering my plan. It was a daring venture, but I knew it was worth trying. If I was caught or killed, I decided even that would be better than watching my family members die from starvation. I was determined to go: it was time to be a man.

Later that day, I sought out the kids I knew who were smugglers. They confirmed the location of the hole in the wall. They gave me advice on when and how to escape. I visualized the path to the farmer's house, recalling the major landmarks along the way. I could not remember the farmer's name; so very casually, I asked my father and memorized his name in case I lost my way.

That night, I waited until my family fell asleep. After one long look at each of their faces, I tiptoed from our apartment and shut the door behind me.

It was an unusually chilly August night, and I shivered as I ran down Twarda Street to the building that housed the hole to the outside. There, I found other boys waiting to crawl through the wall. They were more experienced than I, and they warned me to wait until the last guard passed. Once we heard the guard's footsteps disappear into the quiet, we pushed our way through the wall, and one-by-one, disappeared into the night.

I raced through the dark, ducking in and out of doorways to catch my breath. I made it to the edge of Warsaw without being noticed. Ahead of me, a dirt road stretched into the farm fields. I knew if anyone saw me running along the road, they might question me; so, I made my way into the farm fields and ran parallel to the road, always staying inside the cover of the crops.

CHAPTER 6
"THE NAZIS CAME AND TOOK EVERYONE AWAY"

It was early morning when I reached the farmer's home. From a distance, I saw several wagons and horses in his yard. Light and laughter spilled through the windows. The farmer and his friends were celebrating something.

I tapped on the door, and the farmer answered. He recognized me and came outside, closing the door behind him. I explained the reason for my visit and why it was so late at night. The farmer was not surprised: he seemed to know about conditions in the Ghetto.

"I will help you, but not right now," he said in a hushed voice. "We have visitors. It would be best if they don't see you."

He brought some food and led me to the barn where he said I could rest on the hay. "I'll be back when our guests are gone," he promised.

I was exhausted from my journey, so I collapsed on the hay and fell sound asleep. When I awoke, the visitors had hitched their wagons and were saying goodbye. As the last wagon pulled down the road, the farmer came to the barn. He took me to the house, and his wife made me the most delicious breakfast of eggs, bread, and milk. I had not tasted anything like it for months.

"Well, I better head back," I said when I was done eating.

The farmer shook his head. "No, no, Menachem, you can't leave now. It's broad daylight. It wouldn't be safe." With a sinking heart, I realized the farmer was right. It would be far too dangerous to be out during the day. There would be more traffic on the roads, and I would be much more visible.

"You had better rest today, then you can head back tonight," he said, and I agreed.

That evening as the sun went down, the farmer loaded a large bag of vegetables over my shoulders. He balanced half in front and half down my back. It seemed to weigh more than me when fully loaded with potatoes, cabbage, carrots, and beets.

We said goodbye, and I set off on the long walk back to the Ghetto. The heavy load slowed me down, and the return trip was tedious and uncomfortable.

The sun was rising by the time I reached the Ghetto. I was surprised to find there were no guards in sight. Everything was quiet, but I knew my situation was still dangerous. I found the hole I had escaped through 48 hours before. I put my sack beside the wall, crawled through the hole, then pulled the bulky bag of vegetables behind me. I was so proud and happy about bringing food to my family, that I hummed one of the melodies I had learned from the cantor.

By the time I reached our apartment, the morning's first light was touching the buildings. I climbed the stairs and was startled to find the door to our apartment gaping open. I stepped in and looked around.

"Mama? Father?" I called out. My voice echoed through empty rooms. There was no answer. I switched on the overhead light bulb, and in the cold, white light I saw the drawers from our little dresser were upended on the floor. The few old clothes we had were gone, and worst of all, my family was nowhere in sight.

At first I thought we had been robbed, but we had nothing a robber would want. I wondered if my family had gone to search for me, but why would they have taken all their old worn-out clothes? Finally, I wondered if something much worse had happened. That was when panic clutched my heart.

I wandered through the building and found every apartment the same. Our neighbors were all gone. The building was empty. The apartments were ransacked.

I made my way to the street and looked around, hoping to find someone who could tell me what had happened. The streets were deserted. I looked up, and in the growing daylight, I was horrified to see lifeless bodies hunched on balconies and leaning from window casements. The Ghetto looked like a cemetery, and I could not find a living soul.

My heart pounded, and my head felt dizzy. My emotions spun around and around: Fear. Confusion. Guilt. Desperation. Anxiety. Sorrow. Where had everyone gone? What horrible thing had happened in such a short time? I had only been away for two nights.

I walked up and down the streets of the little Ghetto for several hours. The situation was the same on Twarda, Panska, Sliska, and Sienna Streets. Windows were broken and glass littered the cobblestones. There were no signs of life. It was as if the earth had opened and swallowed all souls.

Suddenly, out of the corner of my eye, I saw an elderly man shuffle around a corner. I froze, shocked to see another human being. He looked like a ghost, and I wondered if he was imaginary; but as he drew closer, I recognized his face. He was a friend of my father's and had often visited our apartment.

The old man's face was gray, and his eyes were wide with shock. He looked confused and frightened. He tried to speak, but he spoke only gibberish. I was desperate for information, but I couldn't understand him. I began to lose patience, when he finally said, "The Nazis came. They took everyone away."

His thin lips quivered, and a tear slid down his cheek. "Within hours, everyone was gone. I don't know where they went."

I felt every ounce of weariness descend onto my shoulders as the horror of what must have happened became clear. My heavy bag of vegetables slumped to the ground. My legs began to shake, and I collapsed on the curb.

"They took everyone—men, women, even children and babies." The old man dropped to the curb next to me. "Anyone who resisted was shot."

The old man and I leaned against one another and wept. I stared down the street before me, still hoping my father would walk up the road; but, of course, he did not.

If the Nazis moved my family again, where had they taken them? If they were at a work camp, where was it? What kind of work could my little sister and brother do? Should I try to find them? Were they worried about me? Were they alive—or could they be dead?

There were no answers, only questions. My only hope was that my family was together and safe. I clung to the hope that they were somewhere with food and decent shelter.

I was lost in these thoughts until church bells from outside the Ghetto walls struck noon. I was surprised so many hours had passed, and it occurred to me that the Nazis might return at any moment. I decided to go back to the farmer I had visited the night before. I knew the trip was risky, but I could think of no other option.

I gave the sack of vegetables to the old man. "If you see my parents, please tell them I love them," I said.

I wondered how the old man had managed to hide and survive, but seeing how frightened and confused he was, I couldn't bring myself to ask. So, I hugged him, blessed him, and said goodbye. Then I turned and ran.

CHAPTER 7
"IT ISN'T SAFE TO BE JEWISH HERE NOW"

I retraced my steps back to the farmer's house. The risk of being caught was greater in the afternoon sunshine, so I carefully stuck to the trees and farm fields, away from the roads. My legs felt numb and my head was aching by the time I tapped on the farmer's door. He was surprised to see me again, and I broke into tears the minute I saw him.

"My family is gone," I sobbed. "I don't know where they are. I think the Nazis took them away."

He nodded and put his hand on my shoulder. He listened as I described the deserted streets and buildings in the Ghetto. I told him about the old man and how we sat together on the curb, wondering where everyone had gone. I asked if he thought I could have saved my family. I asked if he knew where they had been taken. He simply shook his head.

I talked and cried and talked again, until I had nothing more to tell. My sobs ran out, leaving me exhausted. Then, I remembered why I had come back to the farmer's house.

"Won't you please let me live in your barn?" I begged. "I won't be a bother. I'll only stay until my family returns. I don't know where else to go."

He paused and stared at me. I could tell he was considering my request, but then he shook his head. "I am sorry, son. We have a small farm, and I can't afford to keep you." He thought for a moment, then added: "I have a friend who owns a large farm just eight kilometers from here. Perhaps he can give you a job and keep you there. We will walk over tomorrow and ask him. For tonight, you must rest here."

The farmer's wife gave me something to eat. Then, I went out to rest in the barn until morning. I expected to fall into an exhausted sleep the minute my head hit the hay, but when I closed my eyes, my heart raced and my hands shook. The emptiness, fear, and confusion of the day overwhelmed me. I could not sleep.

The poem I had written just two days before was still in my pocket, wrapped around the stub of my pencil. I pulled it out, unrolled it, and read the hopeful verses. They sounded so victorious, full of life and pride. Now, I felt only sorrow and regret. If I had stayed home instead of leaving the Ghetto, perhaps I could have saved my family. Now they were gone. Would I ever see them again?

Fear, rage, and hate welled within me. I vowed I would find out what had happened to them. If they were dead, I would take revenge. I licked the tip of my pencil and added new verses to my poem:

And then they met Death!
No! No! Dear brother and sister,
Death did not go by.
The time has come:
The time for revenge.
And down deep inside,
My heart burns and flames,

Demanding revenge!
Revenge for Father, Revenge for Mother!
Revenge for Grandmother and Grandfather!
Revenge for all the small children!
Revenge for the killing!
Revenge for the patch with the Star of David!
Revenge for each Jew who died in G-d's name!
Revenge! Revenge! Revenge!

Hot, angry tears dropped onto the paper, blurring my writing. I carefully folded the page and shoved it deep in my pocket, then collapsed in the hay and fell into a dreamless sleep.

Hours later, the farmer woke me. His wife made breakfast and sat quietly with me while I ate. She stared at me, and when she spoke, I understood why.

"Menachem, I want to give you a haircut."

I was startled. At a time like this, a haircut was the least of my worries. "Why?" I asked.

"Your long sideburns and cap are only worn by Jews. It isn't safe to be Jewish right now. Before you leave this morning, I want to help you blend in with other Polish boys," she said.

So, after breakfast, she sat me by the fire and trimmed my hair. She rolled the long curling tendrils into my yarmulke and tossed them into the flames. As they burned, I could almost hear my father groan. I was breaking a Jewish law that forbade males to cut the hair that grew on their faces, and the tradition that said all males should cover their heads out of respect for G-d. I felt both guilty and sad, and I began to cry again.

"I know it is hard, Menachem, but you need to understand that Jews are treated as criminals now," my father's friend explained. "The Nazis made it a crime to hide or help Jews. If we get caught, we will be imprisoned—or worse. I will take you to my neighbor's farm today. To protect yourself, to protect me, and to protect him, he cannot know you are Jewish."

I appreciated the risk this kind man was taking to help me. Then he explained another reason to hide my religion: Nazis paid a bounty of 50 *zlotys* to anyone who turned in a Jew, 100 *zlotys* for a Jewish family. That was a lot of money for a poor farmer, but for many Poles, the money was just a bonus. They were happy to turn Jews over to the Nazis for nothing.

"It is time for us to go," the farmer said. "But remember: You must not speak Hebrew or Yiddish. You must behave like the Catholic boys you knew."

My eyes were swollen and my emotions were still raw, but I tried my best to hide my sorrow as we walked together to his friend's farm. When we got there, my father's friend introduced me as the son of a business associate who needed work. He never mentioned I was Jewish.

My potential employer studied me closely. I was small and slight, thin from starvation. I had curly brown hair and dark brown eyes. I was dressed like other Polish boys my age. I spoke perfect Polish, without a Yiddish accent, thanks to my years in public school. I hoped the farmer would think I was just another Polish kid and would never suspect I was Jewish.

The farmer stared at me for so long, I began to feel nervous. Finally he said, "Yes. I can use him."

I heaved a sigh of relief. At least I would have a place to stay.

When my father's friend turned to go, I realized he was the only link I had to my family. I was overcome with a sense of loss when he turned and walked away. I felt heartsick at being left behind, and a tear trickled from my eye as I watched him go. My new employer didn't seem to notice my distress. He led me to the barn and showed me how to lead his cows to pasture. To control my tears, I reminded myself to be thankful that, at least for now, I would have food to eat and a place to sleep.

Over the next weeks, my life fell into a routine and things went smoothly. Then, one day I began to suspect the farmer had heard about the bounty for Jews. He became obsessed with trying to find out if I was Jewish—but not by asking me. The Poles knew there was a sure way to find out if a boy or man was Jewish: we were the only males in Poland who were circumcised. Apparently, he thought he could get a look while I was sleeping, but he never got the chance.

I was half-asleep in the barn one night when I heard the farmer crawl toward me in the hay. Even the smallest creatures make noise when they move through the hay, and a grown man makes quite a rustle. When I heard the hay crackle under the weight of the farmer, I jumped up.

"What are you doing out here so late at night?" I asked.

The dim glow of the farmer's lantern flickered in the corner of the barn. Startled that I was awake, he began to stammer: "I think I lost something out here earlier today. I am looking for it."

My heart was pounding, but I didn't panic: I knew better than to show I was scared. Instead, I answered in my most even voice, "You should come back in the daylight when you can see. You'll never find what you are looking for in the dark."

He was silent for a moment, then he answered with a menacing tone, "You are right. Why search at night when it is easier to see what I am looking for in the light of day?"

He grabbed the lantern and left the barn.

I ran to the barn door and watched him leave through the gaps between the boards. The swinging lantern threw eerie shadows on the ground as he walked the 50 paces back to his house. I felt certain I knew what the farmer was looking for, and I was sure he would try again. I decided not to wait: I would run.

The barn had two doors: one for driving the horses in, and a back door that led out to the pasture. I opened the back door and started to run. It was a moonless night, and I had no sense of direction. I couldn't see where I was going, but I knew I had to run as fast and as far as I could. I ran all night without looking back. I had no idea where I would end up.

CHAPTER 8
HOPPING A TRAIN

I ran for hours, only slowing when I felt the distance between me and the farmer had provided a cushion of safety. I collapsed in the long grass near the base of a hill and fell sound asleep. In the morning, I awoke to the sound of a train whistle. I sat up and watched a small, rickety train inch up the hill. A woman who carried two milk cans walked beside the train. I guessed she was probably a farmer's wife, taking fresh milk to sell in town. She reminded me of dairy farmers who had sold milk at my father's store.

The train conductor stuck his head out of a window and yelled at the woman: "Why don't you come on board and ride a ways?"

"I don't mind walking. I'm nearly to town," the woman answered, easily keeping pace with the slow-moving train.

I had no idea what town she was talking about, or how far away it was, but I knew if I could get on that train, I could rest and get there more quickly. While the conductor was distracted with their conversation, I ran over and jumped on the train.

My luck was over before it began. The conductor saw me and hurried to confront me.

"Where is your ticket?" he demanded.

"I don't have one," I admitted.

"What makes you think you can ride for free?" he asked. He waited for my answer, but I didn't have one. "You better come with me, boy!"

He took my arm, pulled me to my feet, and led me to a shabby car filled with rough and dirty rail workers.

"Sit there," he said, pointing to a spot on a bench between two large, burly men. I sat where he pointed, feeling very small.

It wasn't long before we pulled into the train station. I looked out the car window and saw a uniformed policeman waited on the platform. The conductor invited him onto the train, led him to the car where I cowered, and pointed in my direction. The policeman scowled at me and asked my name. I knew my name, Menachem Taiblum, sounded too Jewish, so I quickly substituted a Polish name.

"Where are you going, boy?" he asked.

"I'm headed to town. I am looking for work," I said in the most matter-of-fact way I could.

"Which town is that?" he asked, peering down his nose.

I had overheard the conversation between the conductor and the farmer's wife. She said she was going to town, but she never mentioned the town's name, so I could not answer. Caught in a lie, my confidence evaporated, and I hung my head in silence.

After several awkward moments, he asked: "Where are your parents?"

"Killed in the war," I whispered. I couldn't tell him the truth. If I said the Nazis took them away, he would know I was Jewish.

He studied me from head to toe. "We received a notice about a boy who ran away from a labor camp near here. He was about your age," he said. "It was you, wasn't it?"

My stomach flipped upside down, and heat crawled up my neck. My eyes locked with his, and I exclaimed: "No, no! You have me confused with someone else."

"Well, we will see. You are coming with me." From his expression, I knew he thought I was lying. I figured it would look suspicious if I refused, so I followed him.

He led me into the train station and asked if I was hungry. Of course, I was always hungry, and I had not eaten at all that night. He gave me a cup of tea and a piece of bread. I thanked him and forced myself to eat it slowly—even though I wanted to gulp it down in a single bite.

By the time I finished, another train had arrived.

The policeman jumped up. He took my arm and led me onto the train. My instincts told me he was not taking me to town, but to the labor camp that had issued the report of the missing boy. Although my heart was beating wildly, I tried to behave calmly so he would trust me.

We settled into a train compartment just as the train pulled away from the station. We were soon moving at a steady clip down the tracks. I waited until the station was out of sight then asked if I could use the bathroom. I knew there was a tiny window in the lavatory, and I thought perhaps I could climb out. I was surprised when the policeman let me go.

Once inside the toilet, with the door safely locked behind me, I examined the little window. I wondered what it would feel like to jump through the narrow opening and fly from a moving train. I felt sick to my stomach at the thought, but even that was preferable to the labor camp that undoubtedly waited at some future stop. I swallowed my fear, knowing this window was my only hope for escape.

I climbed up and thrust my head and hands out the opening. For a moment, I thought I was stuck, but I pushed and wiggled my skinny body until I popped out the other side. I landed on a step that ran the length of the car, and I clung to it as I tried to catch my breath. I wanted to distance myself from the bathroom window as quickly as possible, so I crawled along the step from one moving car to the next. I knew it would not be long before the policeman noticed I was missing, and I was sure he would soon discover where I had gone.

When I reached the last car, I flattened my body onto the train step. I waited until we passed a grassy ditch, and then I rolled off. I hit the ground with a jolt. Stunned, I rolled into the soft, wet grass that lined the ditch next to the tracks. I lay there until the train chugged out of sight.

When I lifted my head, I was dizzy and a little confused. Nothing around me looked familiar. I crawled from the ditch and began to stumble along. Eventually, I came to a road. I looked north and south, but there were only fields rolling into the distance. There were no landmarks in sight. I had no idea which way to turn or where to go.

The world suddenly seemed huge and overpowering, and I felt very small and helpless. Although I usually prided myself on being 12 years old, and considered myself nearly a man, at that moment, I felt far more like a child. I was frightened, lonely, and lost. I wanted desperately to go home, to go somewhere safe, but I had no idea where that could be.

I raised my hand toward the sky, and prayed: "Dear Lord, please don't abandon me. I don't know which way to go. Please lead me to safety. Please protect me from the Nazis."

I knew at that very instant, G-d heard my prayer. I had an overwhelming instinct to turn left, and so I did. Later, I discovered that I would have walked straight into a labor camp if I had turned right.

I did not run into the Nazis, but it took a long time to find safety. I walked day and night through fields and orchards. When I was hungry, I ate what I could find—potatoes, cabbage, and carrots—straight from the fields.

When I came to a farming village, I went from farm to farm asking if they needed a boy for work. The first question the farmers always asked was whether I had legal identification documents. The village *soltys* (sheriff) had told the farmers they could only hire people who had proper paperwork to prove they were not Jewish. If they accidentally hired a Jew, they could be imprisoned, or even shot by the Nazis. When I said I had no identification papers, the farmers always told me to move on.

After asking at every house in the village, I still had no work; so, I began my journey again. I slept under the cover of the crops during the day and hid when I heard a car or wagon approach. I ate what I could scavenge from the fields. If I passed an apple orchard, I had dessert.

No matter how frightening the situation, I always felt G-d's presence. I believed He would lead and protect me. This gave me hope and kept me going until I came to another small hamlet. Again, I inquired at every home without success. As I approached the last house, I saw a wooden sign that read "Tailor." I knew nothing about sewing, but I knocked on the door anyway. A tall, scrawny woman opened the door and glared at me.

CHAPTER 9
WORKING FOR FOOD AND SHELTER

"What do you want, boy?" she barked.

"I'm looking for work," I answered. She frowned as she noted my filthy hair and my dirty bare feet. She shook her head and shrugged.

"Well, come in then," she said. She called out to her husband, who was bent over a sewing machine in the next room: "This boy is looking for work."

The hum of the sewing machine stopped. The tailor lifted his head and came out from behind his machine. "What's your name, boy?" he asked, moving closer.

"Marian," I answered, quickly adopting a popular Christian name.

"Well, I need someone to plow my field, Marian," he said. "Have you handled horses before?"

"Oh yes!" I lied, "Many times." I was relieved he didn't ask if I could sew.

"Do you know how to use a plow?"

"Of course! I was born on a farm. I worked with horses all the time," I lied again. In truth, the closest I had ever come to a horse and plow was riding on a horse-drawn passenger wagon in Warsaw.

"Well, my horse chases everyone away, then turns and comes back to the barn. I need someone who can make her work."

"I can do it!" I said.

He squinted and looked me over. "You don't look very big, but let's see how you do. I'll hook her up to the plow, and you can show me how you handle it."

He led me to the barn and brought out a brown mare. She laid her ears back, glared at me, and snorted. I knew right then she would be trouble.

The tailor rigged the harness and led the mare to the field. He attached a piece of equipment with two handles: obviously the plow. I had never seen a plow, but I was starving and willing to try anything for food and shelter.

The farmer set the plow into the soil. He talked to the horse and slapped the reins. She began to walk, pulling the plow behind her. I watched as the blade carved the earth into straight, even lines.

"Well, that's it! Keep the rows straight," the tailor said, handing me the reins and plow handles. "Good luck with her." Then, he turned and walked back to the house.

I gripped the handles and tried to mimic what the tailor had done. Luckily, the mare wore eyeshades and couldn't see left or right, so at first, she didn't notice her master was gone. I struggled with the plow, trying to keep it straight and even. It was more difficult than it had appeared during the tailor's demonstration. When I looked back, the rows zigged and zagged across the field.

The mare worked hard for two more hours, but once she realized I was not her boss, she turned and raced to the barn, pulling the plow behind her. The tailor, busy at his sewing machine, missed this spectacle, or my job would have ended right then and there.

I chased the horse to the barn where the plow straddled the door, stopping the horse from reaching her food. I gave the horse a lecture, and then led her back to work in the field again.

The next day, the old mare did the same thing: She chased me away and ran for the barn. This time, I saw the tailor watching from the window. My heart sank. I knew what this would mean.

The tailor came out of the house. "I am sorry son, but it looks like I will have to do this work myself," he said. "I'm the only one this stubborn horse listens to. The next village is about 10 kilometers up the road, perhaps you can find work there."

I started walking and found a job on another farm that very day. My half-day experience as a horseman came in handy when the next farmer asked if I knew how to work with horses.

"Of course," I replied, nodding my head confidently. I never explained that the horse had chased me away and run back to the barn. It seemed like a small detail.

"Where are your parents?" he asked. "Why aren't you living with them?"

I remained very calm and told him a story I made up on the spot. I said my father remarried after my mother passed away. I told him my stepmother was cruel, and I had run away. I must have been convincing, because he believed me and put me to work.

In exchange for work, the farmer gave me meals and shelter. I slept in the barn with the cows and horses. I did not mind; they were warm and comforting. My only complaint was that the farmer's wife was stingy with my food: I was always hungry.

Every Sunday, the farmer killed a rooster, which his wife roasted for his supper. One Sunday, when he was away from home, his wife handed me the knife and asked me to kill the rooster.

"I am sorry," I said, "but I can't do that." I sometimes teased animals, but I could never kill one.

"If you don't kill it, you won't eat," she said.

I shrugged. I didn't mind going without meat for one Sunday. "That's okay," I said, perhaps too smugly.

Her face tightened. "I don't think you understand what I mean," she said, grimacing. "If you don't cut the head off that rooster, you won't eat for a week."

Now, I was in real trouble. I had starved for two, or even three days at a time, but I knew I couldn't last a full week without food. I would be dead by the next Sunday.

I didn't say another word. I was not going to kill the rooster, but I didn't want to upset her further. I walked away, scratching my head, trying to imagine how I would survive for a week without food.

I went to the barn and led the horses and cattle to the pasture. This was the Polish custom on Sundays when Catholics followed the commandment to let their animals rest. Along the way, I noticed a field of vegetables. There, I found carrots, cabbage, potatoes, and more. A feast! I pulled several carrots from the ground. I cleaned them by rubbing them against my pants, and then I ate them. Later that week, I made friends with a cow. From then on, I had all the milk I could drink.

Chickens ran free across the farm, and in some shrubs, I found several eggs. I gathered a couple and took them back to the barn where there was a small wood stove to keep the animals warm in winter. With eggs and vegetables, I knew I would not starve; however, I worried that the farmer or his wife might notice that the eggs were missing.

When I cracked the eggs, I was in for a surprise. The shells were empty. I looked more closely and noticed a tiny hole in the shell. An animal had gotten to the eggs before me, made a tiny hole, and sucked the contents out. The empty shell was left intact. I was disappointed, but the empty shells gave me an idea.

The next day, when the farmer and his wife were out of the house, I stole a needle from her sewing basket. I gathered some eggs and did just what the animal had done: I made a tiny hole in the shell and sucked the contents from the egg. I replaced the empty shells where I had found them. If the farmer discovered them, he would think an animal had done the damage. In this way, I began to compete for food with a little animal I had never seen.

The farmer's wife kept her word: She never offered me anything to eat during that entire week. She never asked how I survived without food. The truth was, she never *had* given me enough to eat. Now, I was full and satisfied with eggs, milk, and vegetables.

Every day, I led the grazing animals out to a distant pasture where they ate grass and rested. To provide water for them to drink, the farmer had built several ponds around his farm. Just like the animals, I also drank from the ponds. On those long, lonesome days, the ponds also provided my entertainment.

One day, a chicken strutted out of the long grass near the pond. It was a warm afternoon, and the chicken looked hot to me. Perhaps she would like a dip in the pond, I thought. I knew ducks could swim, so I figured that chickens could swim, too. I grabbed the chicken and threw it into the pond. The chicken began to squawk and thrash. By the time I realized she was sinking, the poor chicken had nearly drowned. I knew if the chicken died, I might lose my job, so I jumped into the water to save her. She scratched and flapped, but I managed to bring her to the shore—wet, but alive.

I repeated the same mistake with a tomcat I found creeping through the grass. I knew that dogs liked to swim, so I thought the cat might as well. I grabbed the cat and threw it into the pond. Turned out, the cat didn't like swimming any better than the chicken. He paid me back one day when I cornered him in the barn. He jumped on my head and scratched me until I bled. After that, I never saw the cat again.

CHAPTER 10

"ANYONE WITH NO BIRTH CERTIFICATE IS A JEW"

I was in the pasture watching the cows one day when I noticed a group of about twenty men walking down a nearby country road. Nazi soldiers surrounded the men, and German Shepherd dogs circled at their feet, barking and howling.

I crept through the long grass to get a closer look. I realized the men were Jews, dressed in traditional orthodox clothing. I wanted to see where they were going, so I followed them, hiding in the grass a safe distance away.

The soldiers led the men to an old wood barn, quite a long way from the nearest village, but not far from the farm where I worked. The soldiers ordered the men into the barn. When the last man was inside, the soldiers swung the doors closed and bolted them shut.

I wondered what they were doing. Perhaps they were going to keep the men in the barn until they could transport them somewhere else. To my horror, the soldiers' intentions were much worse.

The Nazis began to set fire to piles of dry hay that lay on the ground at the base of the barn walls. In minutes, hot orange flames engulfed the barn. Shrieks of agony echoed from inside the barn as the Jews trapped within realized what was happening. I could hear their voices pleading in Yiddish and praying in Hebrew as flames shot through the roof, followed by dark black smoke. A few men pushed through the burning walls, and the soldiers shot them dead.

I could not believe my eyes: This was the worst and most terrible thing I had ever witnessed. Smoke and the smell of burning flesh billowed over the field. I stifled a scream and fought the urge to cough. Bile rose in my throat and I became sick. I hid in the grass and covered my ears, trying to block the sounds, but I could hear everything. Frozen in fear, I crouched there until the gunshots, screaming, and barking grew fainter. It wasn't long before I heard only German voices.

I couldn't fight the urge to run any longer. I bent low in the long grass and started to run. My legs pumped faster and faster, powered by fear and adrenaline. The smell trailed me back to the farm, where I hid in the hay and sobbed. I could not wipe the terrifying images and sounds from my mind.

It occurred to me that the Nazis had arranged to use that barn with the agreement—or at least the knowledge—of a local farmer. That's when I realized the farmers in this area were probably Nazi sympathizers who hated Jews. My stomach knotted with fear.

A few days later, I noticed that the farmer for whom I worked was scrutinizing every move I made. It didn't matter if I was working, resting, or eating, he had his eyes on me. Sometimes, he came to the field and watched me from a distance. Other times, he approached me and asked all sorts of probing questions.

The farm no longer felt safe, but I didn't know what to do. The farm's location was very remote. I had no contacts, nowhere to go, no one to ask for help. Sometimes the sound of my own heartbeat was so loud, it was all I could hear. I tried to remain calm in the farmer's presence, but the vision of the burning barn was fresh in my memory. As always, I clung to my faith in G-d and hoped I would survive.

One morning, the farmer came to the barn while I was sleeping near the horses. He gave me a long list of chores for the day, then he left with the horse and wagon. When he returned a few hours later, he had a large, fierce-looking bulldog with him. I suspected the farmer was planning something, and I was afraid of what it might be.

The next day, the farmer prepared his wagon for a trip to town. Before he left, he called me to a spot near the barn where he had chained the bulldog. I studied the dog's meaty head and drooling mouth. He snarled and barked at me. I expected that the farmer would ask me to feed the dog while he was gone, but instead, he ordered me to sit on the ground near the dog. He took out a rope and tied me to the barn wall. He said the dog was hungry and would attack me if I tried to get away. Then, without another word, the farmer climbed into his wagon and left me there.

I looked at the dog. It was panting and drool dangled from its yellow teeth. When I wiggled, he growled and barked, his ears flat against his giant head. My throat was so tight that I couldn't make a sound. I shook with fear.

As soon as the wagon was completely out of sight, I heard the door to the house open. The farmer's wife came out, and she walked toward me. Her eyes were wide with worry.

"My husband is going to the village to get the police," she said. "Our neighbor told him that anyone who doesn't have a birth certificate is a Jew. If the authorities find out we have a Jew on our farm, we could go to jail, to a labor camp, or even be shot." I suspected that fear was not her husband's only motivation. By informing the police, he could also collect the bounty of 50 *zlotys*.

"I am going to let you go," she said, "but you have to run as fast and far from here as you can. If you get caught, you cannot tell them that I let you go. If you do, I will say you are lying."

She set a dish of meat scraps before the dog. While he gulped at the food, the farmer's wife came closer and untied the ropes that restrained me. She had never been particularly kind to me, but at that moment, I felt sorry for her, left alone to answer to her husband and the police.

"What will you tell him when he comes back and discovers I have disappeared?" I asked.

"Don't worry about that," she answered. "I'll tell him you got loose somehow and ran away. What he is doing is wrong. You could be killed if you stay here."

She told me to run in the opposite direction from which her husband had traveled. She thought it would take several hours before he returned.

I was grateful for this act of courage and kindness. "May G-d bless you and reward you for what you have done," I said. Then, I turned and ran into the fields.

Once again, I ran as fast as I could. Eventually, tired and breathless, I collapsed, exhausted. I sat among the crops and rested.

I was about to run again when I saw an elderly man working in the field some distance away. I yelled to him: "How far is it to the nearest town?" He said the town of Grojec was five kilometers away. When a villager said five kilometers, it usually meant about 10, and sure enough, I walked another three hours before I saw buildings on the horizon.

It was almost dark and the roads were quiet, so I took a risk and followed the main thoroughfare into town. Almost immediately, I regretted my poor judgment. A man in a uniform approached from the opposite direction. I tried not to make eye contact with him, but every time I glanced up, he was staring at me. He never took his eyes off me. I began to wonder whether I had been reported. I wondered if I should turn and run. I was just about to bolt when his eyes narrowed, and he pointed his finger at me.

"I know you!" he yelled.

CHAPTER 11
"THIS IS YOUR NEW NAME – MARIAN REDLICKI"

At that moment, I thought my life was going to end. I had no recollection of the man, and I wondered if he was hunting me for the Nazis or for the farmer. Fear and hunger made me lightheaded.

"No, sir," I said, shaking my head firmly, "I have never seen you before." I broke into a cold sweat, and I thought I might faint.

"But, I know who you are! You're the son of Mr. Israel who owned the grocery store on Panska Street."

Oh no! He does know me, I thought. He knows my father, so he must know I'm a Jew.

I was certain he planned to turn me over to the Nazis so he could claim a reward. My heart sinking, I realized I had waited too long to run away. If I ran now, he or someone else could catch me, so I kept talking and hoped I could discover his plan.

"Where are your parents?" he asked.

"Killed by a bomb," I lied.

He shook his head and asked a few other questions. While we talked, he drew closer. Suddenly, he took me by the arm.

"You had better come with me," he said.

His grip on my arm was like an electric shock. Fear shot through me again. I didn't know where he was taking me, but he had a tight hold, and I had no choice but to go with him.

We walked for an hour around the outskirts of town while the sun set in the distance. It was completely dark when we finally reached a drab building. We climbed three flights of dimly lit stairs, then walked down a hallway that smelled of mildew and old potatoes. He knocked on a worn apartment door. It creaked open, and a tall, skinny woman with a sour, pinched face peeked out. She squinted at me, but didn't say a word.

"Keep this boy until I come back," the man commanded. He shoved me inside the apartment, then turned and left. The woman locked the door behind him, then put the key into her pocket.

She guarded the door and watched me dutifully day and night. I was sure she guessed I was a Jew, and I thought she probably wanted to kill me. She gave me some bread to eat, but I was afraid to eat it. I thought it might have rat poison in it. I never had any idea who she was, or what she would do with me. She never said a word to me.

Where had the man in the uniform gone? I got no hint from the woman who guarded me. I suspected he had gone to inform the Nazis, so he could collect the bounty. I was sure he would return with soldiers to take me away, but it was taking him a very long time.

I counted ten days before the uniformed man finally returned—alone.

"Did my sister take good care of you?" he asked. That was how I found out the two were related. He thanked her, then turned to me. "Let's go," he said, gripping my arm again. I was happy to leave the home of the strange woman, but I was sure the Nazis waited outside. I tried to prepare myself for whatever came next.

The man led me down the dark staircase and through the village streets, his hand locked on my arm. We walked to the far edge of town, and he took me to a dark, narrow alley. This must be it, I thought. More police will be around the next corner. Just when I was sure he was going to hand me over to the authorities, he handed me a Polish birth certificate instead.

"Here, look at this," he said. "This is your new name: Marian Redlicki. Learn it, and don't forget it."

I stared at the certificate and saw a Polish name and a birth date one year older than my real age. It took me a few minutes to realize he was giving me false identification papers! He was saving my life. This was the last thing I expected. I could not believe it: This was my ticket to freedom.

"From now on, your father was Josef, and your mother was Rosalia. Her maiden name was Vedrovska," he said. "Repeat it."

"Josef. Rosalia. Vedrovska." I repeated.

Then he told me how he knew me, and as he talked, I began to remember him. We had been neighbors on Panska Street. He was the policeman who lived in the building where my father owned the grocery.

"Your father was a good, kind man," he said. "On nights when I came home late from work, Israel always let me in through the back door so I could feed my family." He looked away and shook his head. "Yes, he was a good man."

Now I understood why he had done this for me. These documents were a way to return my father's kindness.

"You must practice your new name. Repeat it over and over to yourself," he said. "Forget your real name. Forget your parents' names. Answer only to Marian Redlicki. Forget you are Jewish. From now on, you are Catholic."

He pointed me in the direction of the next town, "Good luck, and G-d bless you, Marian," he said.

I ran off without looking back, my heart filled with gratitude and relief. "My name is Marian Redlicki. My name is Marian Redlicki," I chanted over and over as I ran.

After that, I was no longer a Jew—at least not according to my birth certificate. Now I was a Polish Catholic, with a Polish name and Polish parents. Now I could find a job. Now I could move freely and without fear.

At least, that is what I thought.

CHAPTER 12
WORK FOR FOOD AND MASS EVERY SUNDAY

My joy did not last long. I hadn't travelled far when I remembered I had nowhere to go. I whispered a prayer, asking G-d to guide me. As always, I stuck to unpaved trails through vegetable fields and orchards. When I was hungry, I pulled up a potato and ate while I walked.

By midday, the sun was beating down, and I still hadn't reached a village or town. I continued walking, thirsty and tired. Toward dark, I came upon a hayshed. I peeked in the door and saw huge mounds of soft hay. I crept in, praying the farmer would not find me, and rested there until the morning sun streaked through cracks in the walls. As I left the shed, I said another prayer, pleading for a job and something to eat.

I walked all day and finally came upon a large village. I asked for work at a dozen places before I found a job at a farm. The farmer's wife invited me into her house.

"Are you hungry?" she asked.

I was starving, but I didn't think I should tell her. Instead, I said, "If you have a little something, I would appreciate it."

After I ate, her questions began: What is your name? Do you have a birth certificate? Where is your family? Why aren't you with them?

I produced my new identification papers and recited the information exactly as planned. When it came to questions about my family, I said my parents were killed when a bomb fell on our building. Although it was not the truth, thinking of my parents made me cry, and tears rolled down my dirty cheeks.

"You poor, poor boy," she said, her brow furrowed with sympathy. "Were you hurt?"

"Oh, I was away at the time," I answered vaguely, brushing the tears away. That seemed to satisfy her curiosity, and our conversation moved on.

"What do you know about working on a farm?" she asked.

"Oh, I know a lot about farms. I practically grew up on one." It had become easy to tell this lie.

"It's all settled, then," she said. "We will feed you, and you'll sleep in the barn. During the week, you'll plow the fields. On Sunday mornings, you'll take the horse to pasture, and you'll bring her in at night."

"That will be no problem," I said. "I'll do a good job."

I turned to go, anxious to rest after my long walk. "One more thing..." she added, "Don't worry about getting to Mass on Sundays. You will come with us after you get the horse out to the field." She smiled, certain that she had relieved my greatest concern. It seemed as if all Poles were Catholic, and she was no exception. I nodded and smiled as I headed for the door.

That was that. Every Sunday, after taking the horse to pasture, I walked eight kilometers beside the family's wagon to attend Mass. I had no shoes, so I walked barefoot. The farmer wanted me to wear shoes into the church, so he loaned me an old pair of shoes with wooden soles. Every Sunday, I slung the shoes over my shoulder and carried them all the way to town. I put them on to enter the church, then took them off when Mass ended, and carried them home again.

I listened carefully to the prayers at Mass and memorized them all. Before long, I could recite the *Lord's Prayer* and *Hail Mary* as well as anyone. I mimicked the gestures the Catholics made at Mass, genuflecting and crossing my chest. As I gained confidence, I became more and more convincing. Soon, no one could have guessed I was not born and raised in the Catholic faith.

To prove my devotion, I recited my prayers as loudly as possible, often drowning out the voices of the farmers and their children who sat nearby. I created such a spectacle that the priest once pointed me out as an example to others. As a reward for my piety, he gave me a large cross, suspended on a chain. I wore it around my neck until the end of the war.

On weekdays, I took care of the animals and helped around the farm. As promised, I was rewarded with food. Lunch and dinner were always the same: mashed potatoes and a beet soup called borsht. For breakfast, I got a piece of freshly baked bread. The farmer's wife also made the most delicious cookies, and for a special treat one day, she let me have one. After that, I craved those cookies, but she never offered me another.

One day, the farmer and his wife left for the market and said they would not return until late that evening. The other farm hands took the day off and went to visit their families, leaving me alone.

As the day wore on, my daydreams of those delicious cookies became unbearable. I had seen the farmer's wife making the cookie batter, and I was sure I could remember how she did it. There was plenty of time to bake a batch or two before everyone came home.

I crept into the kitchen, and pulled out a large bowl and spoon. I found the flour and began to mix flour and water into dough. At first, the mixture was too soft, so I added flour. Then, it became too dry, so I added more water. I continued to add flour, then water, until I had a glob of dough so big, it could feed 10 people.

I looked at the huge, sticky ball of dough and began to panic. If the farmer came back and discovered what I'd done, I would be fired. I began to sweat. I regretted ever starting this fiasco. What was I going to do?

I threw the sloppy dough into a bucket, and lugged it to the horse barn. In a dark corner where horse droppings collected, I dug a hole in the dirt floor. I plopped the doughy glob into the hole and covered it with dirt and manure. Along with the dough, I buried my desire to ever bake cookies again.

CHAPTER 13
HARD WORK AND A STUBBORN HORSE

As fall set in, the days grew shorter —and colder. Although I went bare foot all summer, I knew my feet would freeze in the cold, snowy winter without some sort of protection. I asked the farmer's wife for a few old rags, and I tied them around my feet. By the end of each day, the rags were wet and soggy, so at night, I set them near the stove to dry. They were often still damp when I tied them back onto my feet in the morning. Eventually, my toes grew numb. They swelled and turned black. My toenails fell off, but I never lost my toes.

As winter approached, the farmer and his wife decided it was time to make blankets out of the goose down they had collected all year. As often happened in the country, they invited their friends, and they made a party out of the chore.

It was snowing as horses and wagons filled the yard. Girls and women went to work, stuffing goose down and feathers into pillow and blanket casings, while the boys and men entertained them by singing and playing musical instruments. The men had a still, and they made vodka from a fermented mash of potatoes and beets. I carted snow and water back and forth all day for the still.

When the work was done at the end of the day, the farmer and his guests feasted, drank vodka, and danced until early the next morning. I watched from the barn. When I grew too tired, I listened to the noise and excitement from my bed in the hay. I hardly slept before the sun rose.

Near daybreak, the farmer and his friends finally went to sleep, but there was no sleep for me. I struggled up from the hay and wrapped the damp rags around my feet. I shivered in my thin shirt and worn jacket as I fed the horses and led one from the barn. On my way to the field, I passed the farmer's house. I felt wretched and jealous thinking of the young partygoers, still asleep in warm beds with their families around them.

I hurried the horse through the chilly morning air and hitched him to the plow. The horse was cold and tired, too. He refused to pull. I yelled and slapped the reigns, but he stood his ground and snorted at me. On most days, I was patient with the animals, but on that morning, I was exhausted and angry. I grabbed the whip and gave him a lash.

The horse did not like that! He raised his leg and kicked me hard in the chest. I fell to the ground, gasping for breath. Shocked by the blow, my emotions rushed to the surface. My whimpers turned to sobs, and I lay on the ground and cried, not so much from the pain of the blow as from the overwhelming agony of loneliness, desperation, and isolation that I felt.

I struggled to control myself: I knew there was no point in self-pity. I clung to the hope that when the war was over, I would find my family again. We would celebrate with singing and feasting in the traditions of my childhood. I would have warm clothing and a home. I would feel the arms of my mother and father around me. I prayed for my vision to come true, and my hope carried me through another day.

That stubborn horse and I disagreed on several other occasions. One winter day, I took the horse and wagon into the forest to haul wood for the farmer's fireplace. The wood was wet, and by the time the wagon was fully loaded, it was very heavy. I ordered the horse to pull the wagon, but he whinnied and stomped his foot. He wouldn't move an inch. He turned his head and looked at me as if to say, "Pull it yourself."

I tried everything: I talked to the horse. I patted him. I rubbed his nose and gave him a carrot. He still refused to pull the heavy wagon.

This went on until the sun dipped low in the sky. I knew if I couldn't get the horse and wagon back to the farm soon, I would be in trouble. Hot tears of frustration ran down my face. I could not let this horse cost me my job. The winter was harsh, and I would never survive if I were hungry and homeless.

Desperate, I asked G-d for help, and that's when I had an idea. I gathered some brush and started a small fire. Then, I ran to a nearby potato field and dug a potato from the ground. I threw the potato into the fire until it was good and hot. Then, I lifted the horse's tail and slipped the hot potato under it. The shock of the hot potato against his skin, made the horse jump. The potato fell out from under his tail, but not before it did its job. I barely had time to jump on board as the wagon full of wood sailed down the road. I felt guilty for hurting the horse, but I kept my job for a while longer.

The farmer later told me that his horse often acted strange. Many farmhands before me had quit because of this obstinate animal. All I knew was I could not lose my job—especially in the middle of winter.

The horse may have been stubborn, but he was also smart, and he had a fine sense of direction. More than once, he found his way to the barn from the farthest fields. One afternoon, a fierce storm blew in while the farmer and I were driving the horse and wagon home from his sister's farm in another village. The sky had grown black, and rain fell in torrents. The roads became a maze, and every muddy lane began to look the same. The farmer and I sat, soaking wet, on the wagon's buckboard, pulling the reins right, then left, guessing where to go. After an hour, we were back where we started, surrounded by empty fields.

I knew the farmer was frustrated, so I suggested he drop the reins and let the horse lead himself. At first, the farmer thought it was a bad idea, but after we drove in circles a while longer, he took my suggestion. The horse found his way straight back to the farm without any problem. That day, I gave the horse some extra food.

There was a pleasant rhythm to my days on that farm. I had no clock, so my schedule followed the sun. When the sun rose, I went to work. When it dropped behind the hills, I was done. Lunch was served when the sun reached the middle of the sky. If it was cloudy, I knew it was midday when the farmer's wife brought my lunch to the field. The end of the week began on Saturday night instead of Friday, and Sundays were always a day of prayer and rest.

I ate well enough and kept warm near the horses at night. I thanked G-d for the blessings of life. I was content and relatively happy; but once again, change was on its way, and I never saw it coming.

CHAPTER 14

VOLUNTEERING TO BUILD A BRIDGE

A few weeks before my 13th birthday, Nazi soldiers came to the village. They met with the *soltys*—the village elders—and explained that they needed volunteers to rebuild a nearby bridge that had been destroyed by partisans. The head of every household was required to "volunteer" for service, or to send a substitute to work in his place. Trucks were to arrive in the morning to transport the volunteers to the worksite, and in the evening, they would bring the workers home again.

The *soltys* went from farm to farm, spreading the news. He said farmers who failed to respond would be reported to the Nazis. We knew resisters would be jailed or shot as enemies of the Reich.

That evening, when I came in from the field, the farmer gave me the bad news: He had decided I would be his substitute. He was too old to go, and he figured I was young and capable. He said I would get up early the next day and meet the trucks in the village. He assured me that I would return to the farm at the end of the day.

My stomach knotted. The Nazis had imprisoned my family in the Ghetto, had hurt and killed the people I loved, had starved us, and had finally taken my family away. I did not want to work for them under any circumstances, but I also knew I couldn't refuse. If I ran away, I would be caught and the results could be worse. I comforted myself with the thought that, as long as I came back to the farm at night, I would have a safe place to sleep and food to eat. I agreed to go.

Worry kept me awake that night. In the Ghetto, I had seen the guards and Nazi soldiers round up Jewish men and lead them off "to work." They always promised the workers that they would return home, but all too often, they never came back. I tried to shake off my fears. I relied on my faith in G-d and my hope that I would survive whatever lay ahead.

In the morning, I got up before the sun rose. I didn't have to change my clothes as I wore the only the clothing I had. I brushed the hay out of my hair and splashed cold water on my face. The farmer's wife cooked potatoes and borsht, and we prayed together before and after we ate. Then she packed my lunch in a small basket.

"Don't forget to bring the basket home," she said, "You may need it again."

But I would never need it again, because I would never return to that farm.

When I got to town, about 70 farmers—or their substitutes—had gathered in the village square. I was the youngest volunteer, and I joined a group of young men. We made nervous conversation, until we heard the rumbling of truck engines in the distance. The sound grew louder and louder, until two large army trucks roared into the square. The truck doors swung open, and men dressed in civilian clothes hopped out. I waited for the Nazi soldiers, but none appeared. I began to relax. If there were no soldiers, perhaps my fears were unwarranted.

Our escorts told us to climb onto the trucks, so we crawled onto the open truck beds and sat down. The weather was sunny, and the canvas sides were down, giving us a lovely view of the surrounding countryside. After riding for some time, we came to a river where a bridge hung in pieces. The trucks stopped and we disembarked. Our supervisors invited us to sit on the sunny riverbank and eat our lunches. "Does everyone have enough to eat?" they asked. They were polite and kind, and we relaxed and enjoyed our picnic by the river.

After lunch we cleaned the trucks. When it was nearly dark, our supervisors invited us to get into the trucks and take our seats again. We had yet to work on the bridge, and were surprised to be excused after such an easy day.

We climbed on board, and once seated, our supervisors tied thick canvas tarps into place, covering the sides and backs of the trucks. We rode in near darkness for a long, long while. My apprehension grew: I felt something was not right.

The trucks finally pulled to a stop. Outside, we heard dogs barking and men speaking German. Suddenly, the tarp that covered the truck was ripped back, and we discovered it was night and our civilian supervisors had been replaced by Nazi soldiers wearing uniforms. They carried rifles and urged us to hurry off the trucks. We didn't dare to argue.

Most of us were disoriented from the long drive, but as our heads cleared, we realized we had been tricked. We were not in our village. The trucks had pulled through a gate that was now shut behind us. A fence made of barbed and electric wire surrounded us. This was some kind of Nazi camp. It was obvious we were not going home.

My stomach lurched, and I thought I might get sick. Murmurs went up from the workers in the truck: "Where are we?" "What is this?" "They promised we would go home," "My family needs me."

The soldiers did not answer. "Off the truck. Line up there," they commanded, using their rifles to direct us. The farmers, dazed and bewildered, staggered off the trucks.

I grabbed my lunch basket and crawled off the truck. The soldier noticed me and called out, "Hey, you're just a little guy. I am going to call you Chamberlain!" The other soldiers began to laugh, and soon everyone at camp called me by that name. It was much later that I learned that Chamberlain was the prime minister of England. He was a short man, and because of my size, they named me after him.

CHAPTER 15

THIS IS A LABOR CAMP. YOU WORK FOR THE REICH.

That first night, we assembled in an open area near the center of the camp. A Nazi commander stood before us. "This is a labor camp. From now on, you work for the Reich," he said.

He pointed to the barbed wire fence that surrounded the camp. "That fence is electrified, and you will be sorry if you touch it," he paused for impact. "Do not attempt to run away. If you do, there will be serious consequences."

While he talked, I looked around. Rows of sheet metal barracks stretched off in every direction. They looked temporary, as if constructed quickly and with little care. Inside, the floors were bare dirt and metal bunk beds stood in rows. At one end of each barracks was a table and stools.

The camp was located near the town of Uleniec and was one of hundreds of forced labor camps that the Nazis had established to serve their needs during the war. When workers died of exhaustion, illness, and malnutrition, Nazis rounded up more farmers and laborers and imprisoned them in camps like this one. Besides providing fuel, food, and munitions for the Nazi military, the German government leased our labor and made money off our misery.

"Every morning at six, you must assemble here for roll call. You must stand at attention until everyone is counted," the commander barked. "If someone is missing, you will all be punished."

Before the commander excused us for the night, each worker was given a crockery bowl and a metal spoon, a striped uniform, a pillow filled with sawdust, and a thin brown blanket. The blankets, like our hair and clothing, were soon infested with lice. The weather that autumn was hot, so no one needed a blanket anyway. The barracks' sheet metal walls magnified the sun's heat. The barracks were like ovens during the day, and they never cooled off at night. Over the next weeks, many of us slept outside.

The guards told us that if we worked hard, we had nothing to fear. They said we would work in the fields or chop wood. Other times, we would haul coal in the mines or repair roads and bridges that had been destroyed by partisans. In return, we would be fed three meals a day.

Breakfast, a single piece of bread, turned out to be a doughy mess that didn't resemble anything I had ever seen or tasted. Made of sawdust, flour, and water, it tasted like glue. Someone once threw a piece against the wall, and there it stuck and stayed.

For lunch and dinner, we ate watery potato broth that rarely yielded a single piece of potato. Later, I discovered the guards stole the potatoes and sold them on the black market where food was more valuable than gold. We were never given meat or any source of protein.

Once in a while, an inspection committee visited camp. The guards knew when the inspectors were coming and were always on their best behavior during their visits. The guards escorted the inspectors, glaring at us from behind their backs. We knew better than to complain about the food or treatment while the committee was there. That would only lead to trouble. Besides, during inspection, actual potatoes appeared in the soup. We were thankful that, for at least one day, we got something to eat.

Most of us were especially hungry for meat, and we would consider any source. I was in a group assigned to work near the forest one day when we saw a farmer in the distance hauling a dead horse on his wagon. We were so hungry that we begged our guard to let us ask the farmer for a piece of the dead horse for a snack. He allowed three of us—including me—to approach the farmer.

We hurried after the wagon and asked if we could cut some meat from the dead animal. As soon as the farmer nodded in agreement, we lifted our shovels and hacked off pieces of the horse's flesh. We lit a very small fire because we didn't want to draw attention from camp. We skewered the meat onto sticks we found on the ground and held each chunk over the fire for a few minutes. We didn't want to leave the fire burning for long, so we ate the meat while it was nearly raw, then extinguished the flames. The meat was tough and stringy, but to us, it tasted wonderful. We brought some back to share with the others and even offered some to the guard, but he refused to take it.

Our guard that day was an older man. Compared to other guards, he was relatively gentle and kind. The worst guards were the youngest: the Hitler Youth. These 16- and 17-year-old boys were often the sons of SS officers. Instead of carrying their rifles over their shoulders like other guards, they pointed them directly at us, ready to shoot at any opportunity. They were fanatical about proving their loyalty to Hitler and the German Reich.

While we ate that day, one of the prisoners turned to our guard and asked, "Why is it a good day when you guard us, but a bad day when a Hitler Youth is our guard?"

He looked up at the sky and said, "See the sun shining?"

"Yes, of course," we said, thinking the guard was avoiding our question.

"Today, it is sunny, but tomorrow it may rain."

"What do you mean?" one of the prisoners asked.

"Today, I hold a gun at your back, but tomorrow you may stand with a rifle guarding me. When the war ends, if I end up in court, perhaps you will say a good word on my behalf." He shrugged and smiled.

As a work camp, Uleniec differed from the infamous concentration or death camps like Dachau, Treblinka, and Auschwitz. There, people were imprisoned and put to death for their religion, race or politics. At Uleniec, there were no mass murders, but there were still serious consequences for disobeying a camp rule or attempting to escape. Those infractions called for the worst possible consequence—torture, and often, death.

When an escapee was caught, all workers were called to the *Platz de Det* or Death Square. Standing at attention around an open area, we were forced to watch while the guards disciplined the wrongdoer. Those days were the worst days at camp, and they haunted my nightmares.

One morning soon after we arrived, all prisoners were summoned to Death Square. The guards dragged an exhausted prisoner into the yard. They ripped the shirt from his thin back and positioned him between two poles. They tied his wrists to the poles so his arms were outstretched. Then, two guards took turns lashing his back with horsewhips.

At first, the poor man shrieked and cried for mercy, but as the guards continued their torture, he slumped and grew silent. Soon, his back looked like bloody macaroni, and I hoped he was dead so he would suffer no more. A camp officer finally halted the punishment and inspected the unconscious prisoner. Satisfied that the penalty had been adequate, he turned and addressed us.

"If you think you can escape from this camp, you are wrong," he shouted. "We will track you down, and we will find you. When we do, this will be your fate!"

I shook with fear and dread after witnessing this dreadful torture, but it was not the worst thing I would see at camp. The most horrific episodes occurred when a particular Nazi officer came for inspection. We dreaded his visits, because he was both cruel and unpredictable. On one visit, he stood in Death Square with his wife and daughter by his side. Guards brought a woman and her tiny infant into the midst of the assembled prisoners. Seeing a woman at camp was unusual enough, but to see an infant in her arms was especially odd. I wondered what she could have possibly done wrong.

The officer ordered the woman to give her baby to his attendant. At gunpoint, the attendant pulled the baby from her arms.

The officer pointed skyward with his rifle.

I was horrified when I realized what the officer wanted his attendant to do: He was telling him to throw the baby into the air. No, I thought, he can't do that! The baby will die when it hits the ground, but an instant later, the emotionless attendant hurled the baby overhead as if he were tossing a piece of trash into the wind.

The officer tracked the tiny body's flight with his rifle. When the baby reached the height of its trajectory, the officer fired three shots. The baby was dead before it landed in the dirt at our feet.

The baby's mother shrieked, then slumped to the ground in shock. A few feet away, the officer smiled with satisfaction and lowered his gun to his side. His wife was beaming, and his daughter laughed and clapped her hands.

"Again Daddy, again!" she cried, jumping up and down.

No words can describe the sorrow among all the prisoners that day.

CHAPTER 16
A BOY NAMED OLEK – AND OUR ESCAPE

As far as I knew, Jewish prisoners were not taken to labor camps; we were taken to concentration or death camps. Most prisoners in a labor camp were Polish and Catholic. With my fake birth certificate and the cross hanging around my neck, no one ever questioned whether I belonged at Uleniec. I kept the fact that I was Jewish a complete secret.

As the youngest person in camp, I was often lonely and homesick. The camp was a harsh and frightening place. Then one day I met a boy named Olek, and we became best friends. Olek was just one year older than me, and although we usually had different work assignments, we met up in the barracks at the end of each day. We spent every minute of free time together, and we moved our cots so we could sleep near each other. We often talked until we fell asleep, sharing stories about our homes and families. Olek became like a brother to me, and I often wondered if he was Jewish, but I never dared to ask. Not once did either of us even mention the word "Jew."

There was a great deal of illness and death in the camp. People died every day from starvation, illness, and injuries. Lice were everywhere, and their bites often transmitted typhus. Because of malnutrition and the bad food we ate, nearly everyone had some degree of dysentery. The Nazis soon realized that sick or dead workers were useless, so the camp commanders established an infirmary. Seriously ill prisoners were taken there to recover.

A couple of days after I ate the horsemeat, I developed dysentery. When my condition worsened, I was taken to the infirmary. A woman dressed in a long black dress, white collar and black veil supervised the makeshift clinic. She introduced herself as a Catholic nun. She was a kindly woman, and she pitied me, for I was the youngest and smallest person in camp.

When I was well enough to work, the nun arranged a job for me in the kitchen, so I wouldn't have to return to hard labor. After that, I spent 10-12 hours each day peeling one potato after another. It was tedious, but it was certainly better than going back to work in a coal mine. Of all jobs at camp, this was considered the best possible assignment.

I assumed that my role as potato peeler was guaranteed because the nun had arranged it for me. This false sense of security emboldened me, and I began to hide a few potatoes in my shirt every night, smuggling them back to the barracks to share with Olek. It wasn't long before I was caught, and my "guaranteed" job came to an end. I went back to work in the coal mine, and my friend and I survived on watery soup once again.

Olek blamed himself when I lost my job in the kitchen. He apologized every single day we lived in camp. No matter how much I tried to comfort and reassure him, he felt guilty and regretful.

Olek worked in the fields, tending vegetables. As harvest approached, I was reassigned to work there, too. I was overjoyed at spending more time together. Our friendship grew even stronger than before, and we trusted one another completely.

One day, the nun I had met in the infirmary came out to the field on a health inspection. She walked from worker to worker, checking to see if we had any symptoms of disease. She eventually approached Olek and me. She asked about our health and whether we were getting enough to eat. We answered politely, expecting her to say goodbye and go back to the clinic or on to the next prisoner. Instead, she continued to talk about our families and life in camp. We were shocked when she suddenly asked, "Boys, if you had the chance, would you leave this camp?"

We looked at each other in shock. What was this woman asking us, and why? Was she a spy for the Nazis? Was she sent to find out if we were planning to run away? I had visions of the man who had been tortured for trying to escape, and I shivered involuntarily.

Olek and I had no idea how to answer, so we said nothing.

The nun waited a few minutes, then she nodded her head.

"I understand, boys," she said. "You don't trust me, and I can see why."

She turned and walked away, and we breathed a sigh of relief.

A few days later, the nun was back in the field again, asking the workers about their health. She made her way to us and repeated the question.

"Boys, if you could get away from here, would you do it?"

Again we didn't answer.

"I see you still don't trust me," she said. "May G-d bless you both. I will come back again." She turned and walked back toward the infirmary.

Now Olek and I were very puzzled. For the next two days, we pondered the reasons she would ask if we wanted to escape. It did not seem likely that a nun would be a Nazi spy, but anything was possible. On the other hand, we wondered if she might truly feel sorry for us, the two youngest, smallest boys in this hellish place.

Whatever her motives might be, her question opened a window of hope. For the first time, we began to imagine what it would be like to run away from camp—to be free again.

"The next time she comes out here, let's say 'yes'," I said. "What have we got to lose? This is no kind of life, and we will probably die if we stay here much longer."

"But, maybe it's a trick," Olek said.

"I don't think so. The nun believes in G-d," I said, "and she was so kind to me when I was sick. I think we can trust her."

"Even if she *is* good, and she helps us to escape, the guards might catch us and kill us," Olek said. "Remember the man they whipped to death?"

We both grew silent. Neither of us would ever forget.

We continued the debate for several days. The nun stayed away, and we thought perhaps our opportunity had passed. We began to regret that we hadn't accepted her offer of help when we'd had the chance.

Then, one warm evening, we were sitting outside when the nun began circulating among the prisoners. She approached us again.

"Boys, I am going to ask you one last time: Do you want to try to leave camp?" she whispered.

Olek and I exchanged glances, and in the same breath, we both whispered: "Yes!"

Sister did not even blink. She simply smiled and said, "Good. Today is Friday, and Sunday night the regular guards are off duty. They are usually in their barracks drinking, and they won't notice you."

She paused and looked around to see if anyone was listening, then she drew closer. "On Sunday night, pretend you are going to sleep outside again. Position yourselves here, near the fence. I will bring you a pair of pliers with rubber handles. One of you must use the pliers to cut the barbed wire. Then you should hold up the electrical wire so the other can crawl out. Be sure to keep your hands on the rubber, not the metal. Then, hand the pliers to the other person, so he can hold the wires. Whatever you do, do not touch the electric wire with your skin."

She paused, and we nodded our heads, hanging on every word.

"Once you are both out, run as far and as fast from here as you can. Take the pliers with you. Go in that direction," she gestured with her hand. "You will come to a shallow creek. Throw the pliers in the water. That will cover their scent when the dogs come looking. Will you remember to do that?"

"Yes, Sister," we said.

"On Monday morning, the guards will discover you are missing," she continued. "They will bring the German Shepherds and will follow your smell until they reach the water. After that, if you have travelled through the water, they will lose your scent. Now, remember, if you don't drop the pliers in the water, they may be able to trace them back to me, and my life will be in danger." She looked back and forth from me to Olek. We understood the gravity of what she was saying, and we assured her, we would not forget.

She patted our faces and raised her voice so others could hear: "And be sure to report to the clinic if you feel sick." Then she turned and walked away.

And so, the waiting began. The hours dragged from Friday until Sunday. Over and over, we questioned whether it had been a mistake to trust this woman. As always, my faith and hope in G-d made me believe in her. I had heard her praying, and I knew she believed in the Holy Scriptures. Surely she was honest.

Olek was not so sure. For him, the next 48 hours were torture. He was certain the Nazis would kill us simply for our intention to escape. Thankfully, he was wrong.

On Sunday evening, we made our beds outside near the fence. An hour went by. Then, two hours passed. We began to doubt whether she would keep her word, but suddenly she was there. As promised, she pulled a pair of pliers with red rubber handles out from a pocket within the folds of her black robes. She repeated her instructions to us again.

"May G-d be with you on this dangerous journey," she said, then she turned and moved quickly away without looking back.

The night grew very dark. Camp was quiet except for the guards' laughter, which echoed from the barracks where they were drinking. My stomach churned and my hands shook, but Olek and I were prepared to try our luck. The stakes were high. If we succeeded, we would be free. If we failed, we would likely die. Either way, there was no time to lose. Cautiously and quickly, we did exactly as the nun told us. We snipped the barbed wire, then crawled like rats to the other side of the fence.

We removed the makeshift shoes they had given us in the camp and ran as fast as our bare feet would carry us. We never paused to look back, but ran for what seemed like hours. Finally, we heard a stream gurgling in the distance. It was the first sign we might be safe.

We found the little stream and dropped the pliers into the water. Their red handles radiated in the moonlight, and we thought of the nun who risked her life to save us. I sent a prayer of thanks to G-d and asked him to bless her.

We waded downstream and crawled up the other bank. We found ourselves in the middle of a dry cornfield. We ran for a long distance until we were hidden among the tall, brown cornstalks. We collapsed there and rested briefly, but the vision of German Shepherds haunted us and spurred us to run again. There could never be enough distance from the memory of what the guards did to prisoners who escaped.

After an hour, Olek and I began to walk again. We kept going until we found a field of potatoes. We dug up a quick meal and then continued on. For three nights, we travelled by moonlight and slept during the day. We wandered through the countryside, never knowing where danger could be hiding. We were hungry and frightened, but I was thankful that, at least I was not alone. Olek was a great comfort, and whenever we grew sad or frightened, we talked of our families and our childhoods.

CHAPTER 17
HEADED TO WARSAW

At sunrise on the third morning of our journey, we saw an isolated farmhouse. A kerosene lamp flickered in the window. We crept closer and peered in. An elderly couple was sitting at the kitchen table. The man was reading a Bible, and the old woman was sewing.

After watching them for a few moments, I said to my friend, "I think we should knock on the door and see what happens. They are old, and they have no telephone. It will be alright."

Olek agreed. So, we knocked, and the old lady opened the door. She looked surprised to see two skinny, young boys so early in the morning. Without asking a single question, she invited us in. She called her husband to greet the guests who had come to visit at sunrise.

The white-haired man closed his Bible, put his glasses on the table, and shuffled to the door. He said a Polish blessing and invited us to come in.

"Are you hungry, boys?" she asked.

Were we hungry? We had hardly eaten in three days. "Yes, please," we answered.

Before we ate, I recited the Catholic prayer for grace that I had been taught on the farm. The woman gave us each a piece of bread, onions, and a glass of fresh milk. It tasted delicious.

After we ate, the questions began. "What are your names, boys? Where are you from?" the old man asked.

I used the Polish name on the false birth certificate, now worn and stained, which still remained in my pocket. We were wearing the striped work clothes from the labor camp, so we had to admit we had run away. We didn't say a word about the creek and the nun who helped us. We had promised to keep her secret. My friend was less of a talker, so I continued on, saying our families had been killed in the war. Of course, I never let on that I was Jewish.

The couple said they had heard of the camp. They were surprised at how far we had travelled. They asked how we had managed to escape the Nazi's German Shepherds. We were surprised they knew this detail, and we said we were just lucky.

"You boys are not just lucky," the man said, "G-d's own angel must be protecting you. However, you are still in danger, and you must be careful. You should stay here for a while. My wife will make a place for you to sleep in our attic. You will be safer and more comfortable there than if you sleep in the fields."

I was immediately suspicious. Why would he ask us to sleep in the attic when there was plenty of room downstairs? The man and his wife were friendly and kind, but their very hospitality fueled my concern. I didn't say anything just then, but when we crawled into the stuffy attic later that evening, my friend and I whispered in the dark.

"The old man told me he works at a church just a few kilometers from here," Olek said. "Maybe a Nazi or the *soltys* told him to watch for runaways from camp."

"I bet that's why he trapped us in this attic," I said. "Maybe he will go get the police as soon as he thinks we are asleep."

We tossed and turned all night, fretting about the couple's motives, unable to sleep. Finally, we prayed together and asked G-d to protect us.

When the woman called us down for breakfast in the morning, we gave thanks for being safe, even though we were both exhausted. After breakfast, we thanked the couple for their hospitality and went on our way.

We walked for several hours, until we met an elderly farmer and his wife, who were working in the fields. We greeted them with a traditional Polish greeting, "May G-d bless you at your work."

"May G-d bless you on your way," they answered. "Where are you going?"

"We are headed to Warsaw to see if any of our relatives are still alive," I answered.

The man said Warsaw had been bombed, and that the Ghetto was nearly empty. He said the last few Jews who remained behind were planning to fight.

I was shocked that this old man knew what was happening in Warsaw, still many kilometers away.

"I hope you don't mind my asking, sir," I said, "but how do you know all this? You have no electricity, no telephone. Where are you getting this information?"

"We have a small battery-operated radio, and we get information from the partisans near here," he said. "If you are going to Warsaw, you must be careful! It isn't safe there."

The couple invited us to their small farmhouse, where they fed us bread and tea, which they made from leaves they collected in the field. As always, we prayed before and after we ate, and we asked G-d to bless them for their kindness.

Before we left that evening, they gave us bread for our journey. The man found some old clothing he didn't need anymore, and we traded our dirty camp clothes for clean pants and jackets. Once dressed, the old man walked us out of the house and pointed us in the direction of Warsaw.

We walked for three days and nights. When the bread they gave us was gone, we ate what we could find in the fields. Sometimes we stopped at a small farm along the way and asked for food.

Most Poles were nationalists. They hated the Nazis for destroying their cities and for killing thousands of Polish men, women, and children. Many farmers supported the partisans and were Nazi resisters, so we were not surprised to meet another farmer who was a partisan sympathizer when we were about a day away from Warsaw. He also had a battery-operated radio and had heard the underground news. He confirmed that the last Jews in the Ghetto were gathering weapons and planning to resist the Nazis. They had asked the partisans and Poles for their support when the time came.

As we walked the final leg of our journey to Warsaw, Olek and I discussed what we should do. Neither of us knew if the other was Jewish, but we both wanted to fight the Nazis because of our horrific experiences in the labor camp. We agreed to enter the Ghetto and fight with the Jews.

It was dusk when we reached Warsaw. The streets were deserted and quiet. Many buildings were damaged or had been destroyed by bombs. Their timbers stuck out like exposed skeletons and broken, dark windows stared at us like vacant eyes.

We waited at the edge of the city until morning, so we could see where we were going. We talked about the danger we would face by entering the Ghetto. It was an intimidating prospect, but we agreed to go anyway. We found a hole through the Ghetto wall—and climbed to the other side.

CHAPTER 18
WE ARE HERE BECAUSE WE WANT TO FIGHT

The streets of the Ghetto were deserted. Many of the buildings I remembered from my childhood were now piles of rubble. We wandered through the maze of streets until we came upon several young people a bit older than us. We asked where to go, and they directed us to a shelter at No. 24 Zamenhofa Street. I knew the place: My aunt had once owned a print shop near there.

The people in the shelter were surprised when two boys, 14 and 15 years of age, arrived at their door. They asked about our parents and why we were there. We told them our parents were dead. We told them about the labor camp and our escape. We told them how we crawled through the wall to get there, and, finally, we told them we wanted to fight with them.

"What's your name?" someone asked me.

"Marian Redlicki," I said, giving my false Polish name.

"And you? What is your name?"

"Olek Polanski," he said.

From the back of another room, a voice called out, "Those are Polish names. We can't accept them, they are not *Amcha*."

I knew what *Amcha* meant. It was a code name used by Polish Jews to identify one another. Translated, it meant "from your people."

At the same moment, Olek and I both shouted, "I am *Amcha*." My eyes locked on Olek's.

"You are Jewish?" I asked him, and he nodded. Until that moment, we never knew for sure that we were both Jewish. We hadn't dared to tell the truth to anyone—not even one another. We threw our arms around each other and cried.

Our interrogator was surprised. "What's going on?" he asked.

"I never told Olek I was Jewish, and he never told me," I said. "We hid our identities to protect ourselves. Until this very moment, neither of us knew the other was *Amcha*."

"I wondered if you could be Jewish," Olek said.

"And I hoped you were, too," I answered, "but I couldn't be completely sure. It was too dangerous to ask."

We hugged again.

If members of the Jewish resistance were unsure of our loyalty, this convinced them. They welcomed us, fed us, and told us to meet with the group's leader at 18 Mila Street. We thanked them and left, still dazed from our discovery.

Mila Street was not far from where we were, but it was dangerous to walk through the Ghetto. In the gathering dusk, the vacant streets were eerie and frightening. Gone were the crowds of people who once occupied this place. All that remained were ruined buildings, broken windows, and a few remains of people's belongings.

The organizers of the uprising had collected in the sixth floor attic of the building at 18 Mila Street. When we knocked on the door, a young man, who appeared to be in his twenties, came out and closed the door behind him.

"What do you want?" he asked. We could see a gun holster hidden under his shirt.

"We want to join you," we said. "We want to fight the Nazis." The young man was startled and told us to wait, then disappeared behind the door.

A few minutes later, a man with an authoritative scowl came to the door. We weren't sure if he was angry or concerned.

"Who are you?" he asked.

We introduced ourselves. "We want to fight with you," we said.

"What do you mean you want to fight? What have you heard?" he asked. Except for a few partisans outside the ghetto, the organizers thought their plans were secret.

"On our way to Warsaw, two different farmers told us that Jews in the Ghetto were preparing an armed resistance against the Nazis," we said.

I am not sure what he expected us to say, but he continued in a gentler tone.

"Have you told anyone else about this?" he asked.

"Of course not! Who would we tell?"

He looked relieved. He opened the door, invited us in, and that's when the interrogation began in earnest. He wanted to know where we had come from, what our purpose was, where our families were, and on and on.

"We came to help," we said.

"What, you young kids?" he laughed. "What do you think you can do?"

"We'll do anything you ask," we said. "Our families are probably dead, and the Nazis are to blame. We want revenge."

"Okay, okay," he said. "That's enough for today. Let's find you a place to sleep for tonight."

The next day, our interrogator led us to a different room on the sixth floor. There, he left us with an older man we had never met. The man was polite and spoke in a soft voice, calling us "kids." He repeated the same questions we had been asked the day before, and he seemed to know our answers before we even gave them. Apparently, he was checking to see if our comments were consistent. As always, I did most of the talking. I poured out my heart and told him everything. I finished by saying, "We are here because we want to fight."

He was still unconvinced, or so it seemed.

"So, your name is Redlicki?" he asked, looking at me. "And yours is Polanski?" he said, glancing at Olek. We nodded. "Those are Polish names, not Jewish names. I am sorry, but we only accept *Amcha*."

"We are *Amcha*!" we replied. "We told them so yesterday." He knew this, but was testing us. Again, our firm answers convinced him.

"Okay. They are good!" He called to the people in the outer room.

We thanked him, wished him success, and left the room.

The Jews who remained to fight in the Uprising belonged to one of three groups. We fell in with Mordecai Anielewicz, the young leader of the ZOB. Anielewicz was about 20 years old, and most of the fighters were that age or younger. We were assigned to a group led by a 21-year-old man who called himself Mariacki. He did not survive the uprising.

It was late afternoon when Mariacki led us to another building where we met more teenagers, though few as young as we. After introducing us, our interrogator from the previous day gave a short speech. Then, we shared some food and went to sleep on the cement floor of the building.

The following morning, we were shown a few guns and some explosive devices. Our instructors explained how the weapons worked and showed us how to use them. We spent the rest of the day building explosives.

On April 18, Polish informers told our leaders that the Nazis were planning to clear the Ghetto of all Jews within the next few days. We all knew the odds were against us, and our leaders told us we were free to go at any time. However, we all wanted to stay and fight for the honor of the Jewish people.

Olek and I paired up like the other fighters and moved grenades and other explosives into position inside the windows of the tall buildings along the street where we expected the Nazis to enter. There were two of us stationed at each window, and we anxiously waited to give the Nazis a surprise welcome. Passover was just a day away, and we said a prayer that G-d would protect us as he did the Jews who had been led from slavery in Egypt thousands of years before.

CHAPTER 19
JEWS ARE SHOOTING US

Just after sunrise on April 19, 1943, we were told that German and Ukrainian soldiers had surrounded the Ghetto. At 6 a.m., they began to march up the street. They never anticipated any resistance. In fact, the soldiers marched with their rifles resting over their shoulders, and their eyes focused straight ahead. If they had looked up, they might have seen us standing behind the window casings and on the rooftops of the buildings as they passed.

We had no ammunition to waste, so we held our breath and didn't fire a shot until the soldiers were well inside the Ghetto. When they were half way up the street, our leaders yelled, "Fire." Immediately, bullets, grenades, and our handmade bottle rockets flew from the upper windows on both sides of the street, taking the soldiers by surprise. German and Ukrainian soldiers who planned to kill thousands of innocent people that day found that they were the targets. Many soldiers dropped in the street, and those who were not shot, panicked and ran for cover in doorways and alleys. One officer raised his hands to the sky and screamed, "*Oh, mein G-tt! Juden Shisin!*" (Oh my G-d! Jews are shooting!) It was not long before the soldiers turned and ran from the Ghetto.

Our initial success was invigorating, but we knew this was only the beginning. More soldiers would come, and they would come with greater force. They would never stop until they'd accomplished their mission and completely liquidated the Ghetto.

General Jürgen Stroop, the Nazi in charge of the Ghetto's liquidation, was personally embarrassed by the uprising and immediately took charge of the action. He called in additional troops, tanks, and planes—all to fight our small band of resisters who had only a few guns and handmade explosives. We knew we would never triumph over Hitler's powerful army. We were destined for defeat and possible death, but we were determined not to go like lambs to the slaughter.

Our leaders anticipated the Nazi's eventual victory and had mapped an escape route through the Ghetto's sewers. When Nazi soldiers marched into the Ghetto with fuel tanks strapped to their backs and began to torch the buildings, a group of 30 or 40 men, women, and children descended into the sewer to escape. Olek and I crawled down into the stinking hole with them and found ourselves up to our necks in raw sewage, barely able to breathe. We groped our way through the dark, underground maze, wandering for what seemed like hours. The men led the way, their wives and children following at the end of the line. Olek and I stayed toward the back to help the women and children.

"We are almost there!" Encouragement drifted back from the front of the line. The first men reached the sewer exit and a stream of light pierced the dark as they pushed the sewer cover up and peeked outside. When they thought everything seemed safe, they pushed the cover open.

Instantly, we heard gunshots and screaming as German soldiers who waited at the opening fired their machine guns into the sewer. The men who had bravely led us, died immediately. Further back, their wives and children screamed in panic. We slogged away from the sewer opening as quickly as we could, turning this way and that, unsure which way to go in the dark, thick sewage that reached our waists and shoulders. Behind us, soldiers hefted canisters of gas into the sewer. Fingers of poisonous fumes wound through the sewer, choking and killing those who inhaled. Olek and I held our breath and pushed on. Although we had started at the back of the line, we were now at its front, rushing back toward the flaming Ghetto.

Like rats, we crawled out of the sewer and found the Nazis had made swift progress. The buildings were a mass of flames and smoke. The air was hot and the heavy black smoke made it difficult to see or breathe. The leader of our small band of fighters told us to get out any way we could. To attract as little attention as possible, he said to go alone or in pairs.

Olek and I immediately set out to find a way through the Ghetto wall. Ukrainian and Nazi soldiers seemed to be everywhere, making movement difficult and dangerous. Every minute in the Ghetto was another minute that our lives were in danger. So, without further speculation, we ran with one eye looking forward and one eye looking back.

We stayed close to the buildings, darting in and out of doorways. When we finally reached a place where we could escape, we said a quick prayer, begging G-d for his protection. I asked Olek to crawl out first, while I watched for trouble coming from within the Ghetto. He declined and asked me to go first. Without hesitation, I pushed my way through.

There were neither soldiers nor police in sight, so Olek crawled out and we started to run. We raced as fast as we could down the cobblestone streets to the edge of the city. Then we headed south into the farm fields. Once again, we found ourselves walking at night and living off early spring vegetables we found along the way.

CHAPTER 20

WORKING OUR WAY TO THE PARTISANS

In the Ghetto, the resistance commanders told us about a partisan group that lived in the forest near the town of Lazy, more than 200 kilometers away. They suggested that if we escaped the Ghetto, we could join them and continue to fight the Nazis. They said to look for *Armia Ludowa*, the People's Army, which welcomed fighters, food, support, and arms from anyone. They warned us to beware of other Nazi resisters who were anti-Semitic. One was the *Armia Krajowa*, or AK, a nationalist group that limited its membership to Poles.

Olek and I set off in the general direction of Lazy and soon came upon a small village. We went from farm to farm asking if they needed help in exchange for food and a place to rest. We were given bread, but no work, so we walked on.

Further down the road, we found a farmer who needed help with his horse. I assured him I knew all about horses, and I convinced him to hire my "cousin" to help with his cattle. In exchange, the farmer fed us and gave us a place to sleep. We thanked G-d for this blessing of food and shelter.

The farmer brought us into his home. His wife fed us potatoes, borsht, and scrambled eggs. After weeks of semi-starvation in the Ghetto, and only a few vegetables "borrowed" from farms we passed, this was a feast! They told us to come to the house for dinner and breakfast every day. At lunchtime, the farmer's wife carried our lunch to the field.

After dinner, the farmer led us to the barn and gave each of us a blanket. We could not believe how well we were being treated. Could this be real or was it a dream?

We sat up late that night, talking and thanking G-d for an opportunity to rest and eat after the trauma and exhaustion of the past weeks. We knew this haven was temporary. Our luck would run out at some point, but for the moment, our bellies were full and we slept on the sweet, warm hay, covered with soft blankets.

For the next two weeks, I took the horse out to plow each day, and Olek led the cattle to pasture. When the sun was at its peak, the farmer's wife brought us lunch. She visited with us while we ate, then took our dishes back to the house.

One day, she told us her husband had been ill. They had no children to help with the farm, and she wondered if he would ever be able to return to work. When she told us that she prayed for his speedy recovery, we realized our jobs would end, but we did not expect it to be so soon. The shock came one sunny July morning when the farmer told us it was time for us to go. His wife packed bread, carrots, beets, and a bottle of milk into a sack for our lunch. She handed it to us with a prayer that G-d would watch over us. We thanked them both and asked G-d to repay them for their kindness.

Olek and I set off over fields and side roads, watching for signs of danger. We carefully budgeted our food so it would last two days, but when it was gone, we still had no place to work or rest. It was mid-summer, so like the rabbits we saw in the fields, we lived off vegetables growing on the farms we passed.

After nearly a week, we approached a large village. As usual, we stopped at the first house, then worked our way down the street. We had nearly given up hope of finding work, when the owner of a large farm said the girl who usually watched his animals was busy helping his wife in the house. We had a job!

There were lots of animals on this farm, and over the next few weeks, Olek became very fond of a little lamb. The two became inseparable. The lamb ran to him every morning when he got up and rubbed against his arm, bleating. He talked to her as if she were human and carried her wherever he went. He loved his little pet and was heartbroken when it came time to leave the farm. For Olek, saying goodbye to that lamb was like losing a little sister.

My favorite animal was a little pony. Wherever I went, I carried a carrot and a sugar cube for "my" pony. In the morning, she watched through the window while I ate breakfast. The minute I left the house, she came straight to me, waiting for her sugar cube. She followed me like a puppy, even walking to church and back on Sunday mornings. If I stopped to visit with someone, she stuck her head between us, as if to protect me. Like Olek, I dreaded the day I would leave the farm and the pony, for I loved her, and I knew she loved me, too.

The day of our departure came in August. Without saying why, the farmer told us we had to move on. We suspected some other farmer had suggested we could be Jews. So once again, we were on the run, without direction, without food or a place to rest our heads. We had nothing but our faith in G-d and our hope for a better tomorrow.

Our journey followed the same routine: walking on side roads and through fields at night and resting amid corn stalks during the day. We ate vegetables from the fields and drank from the streams.

One night, we arrived at a crossroad with no idea which way to go. I closed my eyes and silently prayed to G-d for direction. I felt His guidance and calmly told Olek, "I think we should go straight ahead."

Olek didn't share the same degree of hope and faith. His face wrinkled in desperation and worry. "How can you be sure?" he asked. "What if that direction leads us right to the Nazis, or back to a camp? They would love nothing better than to report they found and killed two more Jews."

"Well, we can't stay here all night, and I believe G-d wants us to go this way," I said.

In a few days we came to a small village. We no longer asked for work, we simply asked how much farther to the place called Lazy. The closer we got to our destination, the more the answer was the same: "Why would you want to go there? It is dangerous! Partisans hide in the woods near there. It is no place for young boys."

Over and over we answered, "Our parents were killed when Warsaw was bombed. We are searching for relatives who live near there."

This answer always made a deep impression on the farmers' wives. A look of pity would sweep their faces, and most would ask if we were hungry and needed something to eat.

In our most polite voices, we would answer, "If you would be so kind to give us something to eat, we would be most grateful."

The fall harvest was beginning, and farmers shared generously. If we were lucky, we were given freshly baked corn bread, boiled eggs, or a cup of milk in addition to the usual potatoes and beets. I taught Olek how to recite the Catholic blessing at meals, and we always said these prayers before and after we ate. We made a point of thanking the farmers who fed us and asking G-d's blessing for them.

After one delicious lunch, we said goodbye to the farmer's wife and headed down the path. Suddenly, from behind us, we heard her shout, "Wait a minute! Don't take another step!"

We froze in fear. My heart pounded. Maybe she knew we were Jewish, and she was going to turn us in for the 50 *zlotys* bounty.

"What should we do?" Olek whispered.

"Just act calm," I whispered back. "Turn around slowly. If anything seems unusual, let's split up and run," I said.

We looked back to find the farmer's wife running toward us with a sack of food.

"I thought you might get hungry later today, so I packed you a lunch," she said. I am sure the relief must have shown on our faces, but she did not seem to notice. "May G-d's angels protect you along your way," she said.

CHAPTER 21
HE IS JEWISH. WE HAVE TO HELP HIM.

Olek and I had not passed a village for several days. Then, one morning as the sun was rising, we approached a small village and saw a boy about our age leading cows to the pasture.

"Hey, boy!" we yelled. "What's the name of this village?"

"Lazy," he answered.

We could hardly believe we had finally found the town of Lazy! As we drew closer, we asked, "Why are you taking the cows out to the pasture so early in the morning?"

"Because it is Sunday, of course," he said. "I have to go to church later." We rarely had any idea what day it was. We never had a sense of time or location.

We walked along with the boy for a while. We told him we were hungry, and he suggested we go to his house where his mother would feed us. We took his advice, and when we tapped on the door, a tall, thin woman appeared. She was surprised to see two young boys standing outside.

"Can I help you?" she asked.

"We just met your son," we said. "We haven't eaten for almost two days, and he said you might be willing to share some food."

"What aren't you home with your parents where you belong?" she asked.

"Our parents were killed in Warsaw when the building they were in was bombed," we told our now-familiar tale. "We are going from village to village, trying to find some of our relatives."

She was horrified that boys, the same age as her son, had walked hundreds of kilometers from Warsaw. Tears welled in her eyes and she blotted them with her apron.

"Oh, you poor boys!" she said over and over, pulling us into the house. "Of course I will feed you!"

She sat us at the table and placed bowls of steaming mashed potatoes and borsht before us. We recited grace, and had just picked up our forks when her husband came in. He seemed surprised to see us, but he greeted us with a traditional Polish blessing. I waited for the usual barrage of questions, but his wife relayed our story before he could speak.

"If you are looking for relatives, there is a large town on the other side of the forest over there." He gestured toward the trees in the distance. "You'll have better luck there than in this small village."

His wife set a bowl of potatoes before him. While he ate, he added, "Of course, you must be very careful in the forest. Partisans hide there. They carry guns and are quite dangerous."

"How do you know about these partisans?" I asked.

"Sometimes I visit a friend who lives on the other side of the forest. I see them when I drive my carriage through the trees," he said. "My friend told me they come into his village to ask for food."

"Do you know how many groups of partisans live there?" I asked.

"No, nobody knows."

"How deep is the forest?"

"Where the road crosses, only four or five kilometers. It is not that deep, but it is wide. It stretches perhaps 100 kilometers," he said. The road through the forest is windy and narrow. You can't see very far ahead, so most people are afraid to go in there."

When we were done eating, we thanked them both for breakfast and the information. The boy's mother packed some food and gave it to us.

"G-d bless you for your kindness and advice, and G-d bless your son for telling us where you live," we said. Then we hurried off toward the trees.

Just as the man had described, a trail at the edge of the forest led straight into the undergrowth, then curved to the right and out of sight. It was so narrow and overgrown, we were uncertain if it was a path for animals or humans. We had no idea what might lie ahead, and it took all of our courage to walk into the dim woodland. The risk of confronting the wrong group of partisans grew with each step. We reminded each other that if we found the right group—the People's Army—we could continue to fight the Nazis. We put one foot in front of the other and kept walking.

The man in Lazy was correct: The forest was very wide. Smaller trails led off from the main path. In case we needed to find our way back, we marked the way by scratching the tree trunks and throwing branches into the path.

On the first day, the only sounds we heard were our own footsteps and the singing of birds, but as we walked deeper into the woods on the second day, we heard moaning. We froze and listened closely. Was someone injured, or was this a trap? As quietly as possible, we crept through the trees. Up ahead, an old man was lying on the ground, moaning, crying, and praying aloud in Hebrew.

"He's a Jew," I whispered to Olek. "We have to help him." We crept closer and the old man opened his eyes and looked at us, his face knotted in fear and confusion.

"Don't be afraid, old man," I said. "We are Jewish, too."

In short, halting sentences, he rasped, "Nazis came to my village and began to shoot. Everyone ran. I was separated from my family.

I lost them. I ran to the forest, and then I got lost." He paused, exhausted from the effort of speaking.

"How did you get hurt?" I asked.

"My family and I were starving. We hadn't eaten for a week," he said. "I've been wandering here, without food or water for I don't know how long. I fell, and I didn't have strength to get up." He began to cry in dry, hacking sobs. "I will die here. I am too weak to go on. I have been praying that the animals will wait to eat my body until after I am dead."

We tried to encourage him to rise and walk with us, but he was clearly too weak and dehydrated. We had no water or food to share. The situation seemed hopeless.

Then, I remembered something I had learned on the farm. "If only I had a knife, I could get sap from the maple trees," I said to Olek. "We always made syrup from trees like these near the farm."

"Reach in my pocket," said the old man, "I have a knife." Sure enough, he had a small pocketknife deep in his coat pocket.

"That's it!" I said. "Come on, Olek!" My friend and I ran to a maple tree, leaving the old man lying on the ground.

Using the man's pocketknife, I cut through the bark. The sap began to run, and Olek and I grabbed giant maple leaves to catch as much as we could. We ran back and forth, back and forth, from the man to the tree, from the tree to the old man. We supported his head and helped him drink until he was able to sit up, and finally, with our help, to stand.

With the old man supported between us, we began walking slowly back down the trail, retracing our steps to the village. When he grew weak, we stopped, cut into another maple, and drank the sap. We traveled like this until we came to the edge of the forest. Before entering the village, we told the old man to hide the Star of David that hung around his neck.

"If they ask your name, give them the name of some Pollack you know. It is the only way to survive," we said. "The Nazis pay 50 *zlotys* for any Jew who is turned in, so don't let anyone know you are Jewish." The old man had never heard this. He had been living in a small village where, until the prior week, the Nazis had ignored the few hundred Jews who lived there.

As always, Olek and I went from house to house, farm to farm asking for work. Most of the farms were very small. If the farmers didn't need help, we asked for food.

Eventually, we found a farmer who was kind enough to let the old man rest in his barn. The farmer said he would take the old man to a larger town when he went to the market in a week's time.

The old man seemed relieved, and so were we. Olek and I were anxious to find the partisans as soon as we could, and we told the old fellow of our plan.

"You must go on without me," he said. "Leave me here where I can rest."

"Are you certain you will be alright?" we asked.

"I would have died without your help. When you found me, I was lost and broken. My family was gone. I was starving and praying that the animals would wait until I was dead before they ate me. I owe you boys my life." He offered us the gold Star of David that was hidden beneath his shirt. We thanked him, but refused. We knew someday he might need to sell it to survive.

Before we left, the farmer warned us about the dangerous partisan groups that carried guns and hid in the forest. We never admitted we were looking for those very fighters.

CHAPTER 22
DO EITHER OF YOU BOYS KNOW HOW TO USE A GUN?

Olek and I made our way back to the forest. We had been searching for partisans for several days, when we heard a rustle in the bushes. We hid in the trees and waited to see if an animal or human would appear. Two young men with rifles slung over their shoulders emerged from the underbrush. Neither wore a uniform, so we knew they weren't soldiers. We decided these must be the partisans.

We stepped out from behind the trees. As soon as they saw us, the young men whipped their rifles into position and shouted, "Hands up!"

We raised our hands, and they approached us. They were younger than we had expected—not much older than ourselves.

"Who are you and what are you doing here?" one of them asked. As always, I was the one to talk.

"The Nazis killed our families in Warsaw," I said. "We have no relatives left. We are looking for the partisans. We want to join the resistance."

They looked us over and shook their heads. "A nice answer," one of them said. "The question is: Are you telling the truth? I hope so, for your sake."

"What I am telling you is true," I said. "We aren't spies. We were not sent by anyone. We just want to fight the people who killed our families."

They seemed to believe us and said they would take us to their "headquarters." One fellow led the way, the other followed behind us, and we headed down the path. We walked for a couple of hours, following markers that only the men recognized, until we reached "headquarters." There, in a clearing, was a small green tent covered with tree boughs so it blended with the surrounding forest.

An older man approached, and our escorts introduced us. The questions began immediately, and we repeated our story. The young men listened and nodded, indicating our stories were consistent with what we had told them earlier.

I was usually moved to tears when I answered questions about my family, but in front of the partisans, I knew I had to be strong. If I cried when I explained that my family was gone, they would think I was too weak. I had to put my past behind me and concentrate on the goal of avenging my family.

My story must have satisfied the man, because he told our escorts to take us to meet other young men who were part of their group. These men were older than Olek and I, but they treated us kindly. We came to a tent where large rocks and tree stumps served as seats. We sat with the partisans and ate our dinner out of metal mess kits, the kind they used in the military.

At first, we thought this was the full contingent of partisans, but we were told that resistance fighters spread throughout the forest. We would never know exactly how many partisans there were.

When the meal was over, some of the men left camp. We were told to stay behind. We were not allowed to ask questions. Eventually, two men with rifles told us to follow them, so we walked for about an hour, until the trees became so thick we could barely move. We struggled through the underbrush to a cave made from branches and tarpaper. The floor was grass. The men with rifles told us to crawl in and rest there for the night. We dared not ask a single question. We crept into the cave and lay down on the grass, using boughs for our pillows. One man sat near the opening of our cave. The other stood guard a few yards away. After a few hours, they switched places.

Neither Olek nor I could sleep. By daybreak, we were exhausted. We finally nodded off as the sun was rising. Almost immediately, we were awakened to move to another location for breakfast.

At breakfast, the men explained that partisans never fought openly. Instead, they sabotaged Nazi efforts by destroying railroads, bridges, and roads. "Today, you will see what we mean," they said. We were told to follow two men we had never met. Without question, we followed for several hours, until we came to a railroad track.

"See that piece of track?" one man asked. "It carries Germans to the front. Injured Nazis return on that track over there," he said, pointing. "Our job is to stop them."

Olek and I nodded in agreement.

"Today, we will show you how to set dynamite. When a train passes—if everything goes as planned—the track will blow. Do you have any problem with that?"

Without hesitation, I said, "I'll do anything to stop those murderers." Later, I learned that my answer to this question cemented the partisans' trust.

The men told us to watch everything they did. They dug a hole under the tracks and jammed dynamite into place. Job done, we turned and walked back the way we came.

"By tomorrow morning we will know if our hard work paid off," one of the men said.

Olek and I said nothing. We followed our teachers back to camp where two of the men were distributing food they brought from a nearby village. We sat on the ground and visited while we ate. The partisans' conversations were always very general. No one ever shared specific information about their actions, and no one ever used their real names. This was for everyone's protection in case someone was captured by the Nazis.

When the meal was over, one of the men asked, "Do either of you boys know how to use a gun?"

Together, Olek and I answered, "No." Of course, we had learned how to shoot a gun in the Ghetto, but we thought it would make the partisans curious if we admitted it. So we kept our Ghetto experience a secret.

"Didn't you ever play with a toy gun?" he asked.

"No. Our parents gave us books, not guns," I answered.

Over the next few hours, we learned how to handle, clean, load, and shoot rifles. Once we could demonstrate adequate skill, we were each given a rifle of our own.

Olek and I were so absorbed in learning about our rifles that we forgot all about the dynamite we had helped to set earlier that day. The sun was setting when we heard the distant sound of a train, followed by an explosion. The men we had worked with that morning whispered that our work had been successful. Olek and I exchanged glances, but nothing more was ever said about it.

One of the leaders told us we would be given our first assignment in the morning. We lay awake all night, wondering what we would be asked to do and how dangerous it would be.

CHAPTER 23
LOSING A FINGER IN A NAZI RAID

At daybreak, Olek and I followed two partisans through the forest for what seemed like several hours. Eventually the forest thinned, and we found ourselves on the bank of a river.

"See that river?" one man asked. "Two men come up the river every day. They are German spies, and we want this to be their last trip. You will hide here in the brush and watch for their boat. Then, you must kill them."

"When will they get here?" I asked, keeping my voice as steady as possible.

"We don't know exactly, but it will be sometime today. You have to stay alert and catch them by surprise. They will undoubtedly be carrying weapons. If you don't succeed in killing them, they will surely come after you," he said. "After you have shot them, run back the way we came as fast as you can. Even if you manage to hit them, there could be a second boat. So, be sharp!"

Our leaders turned and left us standing in the brush on the riverbank. Olek and I crouched low in the bushes, loaded our guns, and pointed them in the direction of the river. Then we waited, and we waited, suddenly aware of how dangerous our situation was. We had minimal experience with rifles and no experience shooting at spies traveling on a river. Although we never admitted it out loud, I am sure Olek and I both questioned what we were doing there. I also began to wonder whether I could really shoot and kill another man, but as the minutes ticked by, my mind filled with memories. I saw Nazis brutally hurting my friends and relatives. I recalled horrors from the work camp, and remembered buildings burning in the Ghetto fire and good men and women dying in the sewers. My heart filled with sorrow and rage, and my fear dissipated. I would do everything I could to stop these murderers.

A couple of hours passed, and our arms grew numb from holding the heavy rifles. Olek and I were beginning to lose focus when a small boat appeared in the distance.

"Look! Look! There it is!" Olek whispered. The boat was barely visible around the bend in the river, but we began to shoot anyway. The water splashed as our bullets hit the water. The men on the boat were surprised and took cover. Within seconds, they were back up, with rifles pointed in our direction. We didn't wait to see where their shots would land. We turned and ran.

Olek and I raced along the path and were surprised to find the partisans who originally led us waiting a safe distance away. They said they had stayed nearby as backup in case the men chased us, but I wondered if the whole "mission" had been a test to see if we would do the job—or simply run away. Perhaps our targets were not even spies. Maybe the partisans used the men in the boat as a way to test our commitment. I was suddenly nauseated, wondering if I might have been shooting at innocent men. Then I realized that the boat was so far away, and we were so inexperienced, it was unlikely that any of our shots would have ever done any harm.

After this test, our fellow partisans treated us with greater trust and respect. They assigned us to perform various acts of sabotage. We set dynamite under railroad tracks. We helped to blow up bridges. We cut telephone lines. We did anything that would keep the Nazis from reaching their destinations or accomplishing their objectives.

The winter of 1943 blew in, harsh and cold. We had minimal shelter or clothing. This limited what we could accomplish. We spent most of our time trying to keep warm in our tents. When the snow finally began to melt, and the days began to grow warmer and longer, we went back to our "work" with renewed energy.

One spring day, a farmer from a nearby village told us that the Nazis knew the location of our camp and were preparing a raid. We knew this meant there was probably a traitor within our group, but we didn't have time to find out who it was.

At daybreak on the day of the anticipated raid, our leaders assigned each of us to positions throughout the forest so we could defend ourselves when the Nazis came. Being small, Olek and I were sent into the trees with automatic rifles. We climbed up among the branches and braced our legs to hold ourselves steady. We waited there for the order to shoot.

Within an hour, soldiers in green uniforms walked up the path. They held rifles, pointed straight ahead, ready to shoot. Our leaders waited until the soldiers were below us, then gave the order, "Fire!"

Our guns blasted at the soldiers from above. They anticipated a surprise attack, but never expected us to be ready for them, let alone shooting from the treetops. The racket of the guns, and the shrieks of injured soldiers echoed through the forest. In retaliation, the Nazi soldiers threw grenades left and right and up into the trees. We continued to shoot through smoke, fire, and explosions.

It wasn't long before the Nazis turned and ran, leaving the soldiers who had led the attack lying in the path below us, dead or wounded. When the fighting stopped, we looked around. A piece of shrapnel had hit my left hand, but I did not feel anything. I realized that my pointer finger was missing, and several other fingers were also damaged. My hand was bleeding profusely, and I saw that Olek, who sat in the tree next to me, had lost the toes from his right foot. The tree limbs were covered with what looked like worms. When I looked closer, I saw they were pieces of human tissue.

We dropped out of the trees, screaming in shock. As the adrenaline began to reside, we began to feel the pain as well. One of the partisans washed our wounds with alcohol, which stung and made them bleed even more. Then he covered our bloody stumps with pieces of salted bacon. The bacon fat staunched the flow of blood, and the salt kept the wound free of infection, but it hurt like hell. He tore a piece of cloth from his sleeve and tied it over our wounds to hold the bacon in place. It was primitive, but it was the best he could do. We could not seek real medical care, because the Nazis required doctors and hospitals to report all injured patients. Later that afternoon, I found my finger under a tree. It was no longer of any use to me, so I buried it there in the forest.

We expected the Nazis to return in greater force to finish us off, so we struck camp and headed into the forest, a limping, ragtag group. Our injuries made it awkward to move. We carried what we could, and we walked for many hours in the woods, winding back and forth to obscure our trail. We were not only watchful for Nazis, but for other partisans as well. There were many partisan groups roaming the forests at the time, and most were likelier to kill strangers than to greet them as friends. This may have been to our benefit: the Germans were just as nervous in these dangerous woods where they could be ambushed and killed at any time.

We finally pitched camp in another place, and resumed our work. Members of our group continued to visit partisan sympathizers in the nearby villages. These supportive farmers and private citizens lived in the country or small villages and provided food and information. They used battery-operated radios and always had the latest news about the war.

The farmers told us the Nazis frequently knocked at their doors, asking about suspicious individuals or groups. They said the Nazis suffered on the Russian front. They were poorly equipped to tolerate the freezing Russian weather. In the winter, more died from exposure than from battle wounds. Every day, trains filled with injured and frostbitten Nazi soldiers headed back to Germany.

We resumed the sabotage we had undertaken before the attack. In groups of two, we ambushed German trucks on their way to the Russian front, and we destroyed bridges, roads, and train tracks.

Another winter was approaching, and again, survival grew difficult. Food, shelter, and clothing were scarce. Because we suspected that someone in our group was a double spy, we relocated our camp again and again.

It was difficult, but Olek and I had faith that the war would end soon. We never knew if anyone else in our group was Jewish, or shared our faith in G-d, but we managed to pray silently and maintain our beliefs. We could make no other choice but to go on with our lives and hope for the best.

CHAPTER 24
THE WAR IS OVER!

At last the snow melted, and the weather began to warm. Our injuries began to heal, and it was easier to get around. Olek and I asked permission to walk to a nearby village to ask for food.

We approached town cautiously and knocked on the door of a known sympathizer whom we had visited many times before. When he opened his door, the man's eyes widened in surprise.

"What are you doing here?" he asked.

"We wondered if you could share some food," we answered.

"No. No," he laughed. "I mean, what are you doing here? The war ended three days ago. The Germans surrendered. The war is over!"

We stood on his doorstep, shocked and disbelieving.

"Are you joking?" we asked.

He continued to laugh. "I am not joking. It is true. It's all over. You can go home!"

Olek and I looked into each other's eyes. Could it be true? Could the war really be over? The pain, the suffering, the loss, the fear flashed before us, then drifted away. We shook our heads. We could not believe it.

We took the food the farmer offered and hurried back to camp. Other members of our group returned with food from other villages. They had heard the same news. We raced back to camp to share the information at headquarters.

When we reached camp, our fellow partisans gathered around. "It's a trick!" our leaders said. "You can't believe anyone. Tomorrow we will verify the information, but until then, everyone must remain at their posts."

The next day, several of our leaders headed out to check out the news with their trusted sources.

Two days later, they roared back to camp. "It *is* true!" they announced. "The war is truly over!"

A roar went up among the partisans that could be heard throughout the forest. They were overjoyed. The Nazis were defeated, and everyone could go home. Olek and I celebrated into the night with our fellow fighters. We sang, hugged each other, and wished each other a safe return home. Our friends talked about their families and their dreams for the future now that the war was over.

Although we celebrated with the others, Olek and I did not share the others' joy. Our situation was very different. Most of the partisans would return to the life they left behind before the war, but Olek and I were fairly sure our families, relatives and friends were gone. We knew our homes had been destroyed, and we had no place to go. It was still not safe to let anyone know we were Jewish because anti-Semitism was still rampant. We were alone in the world.

The more our friends talked of the future, the more Olek and I were reminded of the past. While our fellow partisans had fought to preserve their way of life, we had been fighting to avenge the destruction of our people.

Olek and I were still afraid to reveal the secret we had kept so long: that we were both Jews. We had never once revealed our true identities, and we would learn soon enough that, even though the war was over, it was still not safe to be Jewish.

As we broke camp for the last time, our commander told us to travel alone or in pairs, because larger groups would attract attention. The country was still filled with Nazis who had not yet returned to Germany, and they were dangerous. Although many had shed their uniforms, they still carried their guns. Until the Nazis were gone, the roads were still dangerous.

Before we left, we handed our guns back to our leaders, who returned them to their sources. I found it very difficult to part with my gun. For months, it had been my security, my protector. I slept with it by my side, and it saved my life more than once. Even years later, when awakened suddenly, I would reach under my pillow for a gun that no longer existed.

While the other partisans were anxious to leave, Olek and I were in no hurry. We decided to help collect and return the weapons. Staying with our partisan leaders provided us with some protection and demonstrated our solidarity. We hoped travel would be safer in a few days.

After the weapons were collected and accounted for, Olek and I set off toward Warsaw once again, this time to see if we could find any living relatives. We bid farewell to those who still remained in camp and wished them a safe return home. Our commander drew a sketchy map of the route to Warsaw on a scrap of paper, and we left the forest for good. He advised us to ask for rides only from farmers driving a horse and wagon. He said anyone driving a car or truck might be a Nazi or Nazi sympathizer.

We trudged a few kilometers down the road and became exhausted. I realized that Olek and I were in no condition to start the long journey to Warsaw. After months of living in the wild, we were malnourished, poorly rested, and physically worn from exposure to the elements. I had a plan that I shared with Olek.

"Let's go back to the farmer who gave us food for the group and ask if we can rest in his barn for a week or two," I said. "I bet he will give us some food and a place to sleep in exchange for work."

Olek agreed, and we did just that.

The farmer and his wife were very kind. They happily accepted our offer. We maintained our false identities, and because they were devoted Catholics, we joined in saying prayers and grace before and after meals.

We ate our meals in their house. They apologized for our sleeping arrangements, but they had no children and their small house was not big enough for more people. They offered their attic, but it was stuffy and dark. We were very pleased to share the comfort of soft hay with the animals in the barn.

After two weeks, we had a little more strength and were ready to begin our journey. It was early summer when we told the farmer we would depart the next morning. It was difficult to leave the safety of the barn and the hot, filling meals at their table, but we knew we had to begin searching for our families.

Before we left, the farmer and his wife gave me and Olek some of the farmer's old clothes and they packed food for our trip. They blessed us and wished us peaceful travels protected by angels. In return, we blessed and thanked them for their hospitality and for all the care they had given us.

Olek and I set off, following the crude map provided by the partisan commander. Now that the war over, we no longer had to hide amid the crops. We could walk down the road in the daylight, and only took cover when we saw a truck or car approaching. Olek's foot still hurt, so we walked slowly until the sun began to set. Fortunately, we saw a farmer driving home with his horse and wagon. We flagged him to a stop and asked about the closest village.

"It's about two hours from here," he said. "I am going that way, why don't you hop in the wagon, and you can ride with me?"

As we rode along, we told him our plans to go to Warsaw to look for relatives who might have survived the war.

"My son left home more than a year ago. Went to fight with a partisan group," he said. "Perhaps you ran into him?" He told us his son's name, but of course we had never heard of him because partisans never used their real names.

"I still don't know if he is dead or alive," the farmer shook his head. He drove in silence for several minutes before continuing: "It has been hardest on my wife. She fears the worst. She thinks our son may be dead or injured somewhere. There is no way to find out. I told him not to go. He was my only child, my only son," the farmer's voice caught and he shook his head again.

"I told him we needed him at home to help us. But he wouldn't hear of it. He was determined to fight. Stubborn…stubborn," he shook his head again. "Now, he is probably dead in the forest somewhere. What a waste! What a loss!"

We rode in silence, the farmer wiping his eyes from time to time. We had gone several kilometers when the farmer brightened. "You know, I have an idea!" he said. "Why don't you boys stay with us for awhile? My wife and I are older, and the work on our farm is piling up. You could help us for a bit and live in our son's room."

We weren't sure if the farmer made this suggestion because he actually needed help, or because he thought our presence would distract his wife from her sorrow. Either way, we were starving and tired. His offer meant food and shelter, so we gladly accepted.

When we arrived at his house, the farmer's wife was overjoyed to see two young boys, about the age of her son. She gave each of us a motherly hug. When she let go, there were tears in her eyes. I am sure she was thinking of her own son, wondering where he was that very night and whether he had a safe place to sleep.

"Where are your families, boys?" she asked. He husband told her we were on our way to Warsaw to look for surviving relatives.

"Well, you boys can stay here for as long as you want," she said. "Our son isn't here, and we would be happy to have you."

That night, we sat around the table and enjoyed dinner as a family. The couple talked of their son, his childhood, and how much they missed him. When it was time for bed, the woman led us to her son's bedroom. "Here you will sleep, my children. Good night and may G-d's angels protect you," she said.

It was the first night in years that Olek and I had enjoyed a real bed, inside of a real home, but we could not sleep a wink. We lay awake whispering about the poor woman's suffering. She was kind and caring. She missed her son desperately and hoped he would come home safely, but we suspected she would never see him again. If he were alive, he would have surely contacted her by now.

"We remind her of her son," Olek said. "When we leave, she'll feel as if she has lost him all over again."

Our hearts went out to her. She reminded us of our own mothers, and we wondered if our mothers were alive and whether they missed us and worried about us, too. For three years, we had tried to keep the overwhelming feelings of loneliness and longing for our parents under control.

"I almost forgot what it was like to have a mother," I whispered, my voice breaking. "Why would any son purposefully leave his mother behind?"

We were silent for a long time. "It will be hard to leave here," Olek said, "but I think we better not stay. It will only make it more difficult for everyone." We fell asleep that night with heavy hearts.

Olek and I rose with the sun and had breakfast with the farmer and his wife.

"Why don't we get started on some chores right after breakfast?" said the farmer. His wife looked at us hopefully. I had to turn away when I told her of our decision.

"Olek and I have reconsidered your offer. It was so kind of you to invite us to stay, but we think we better get on our way," I said. "We will have a better chance of finding our relatives if we get started soon."

The silence that followed was more powerful than words. I could not look at the farmer's face—and certainly not at his wife's—without crying. Olek and I got up and prepared to leave as quickly as possible.

At the door, the farmer's wife hugged us both. She was openly weeping. "I wish you could stay," she said. "I know you want to look for your families, but please, be safe. Let no harm come to you." The poor woman was talking to us, but we knew she was really speaking to her own son.

"Please write to us and let us know you are safe," she said. We promised we would, and she promised to let us know if her son came back, but I knew we would never stay in touch. Most farmers were illiterate and required the help of a postal clerk in the nearest village to transcribe or read their letters. This would cost food or money in exchange. So, with their blessing, and a large bag of food for the trip, we set out on a 10-hour walk to the next village.

CHAPTER 25
A SENSE OF PREDICTIBILITY AND NORMALCY

Olek and I were exhausted by noon. We collapsed by the side of the road, nibbling on the lunch the farmer's wife had packed. We watched wagons and trucks pass by. Most were worn and dirty, so it caught our attention when a well-maintained wagon, pulled by a matched pair of beautiful, brown horses approached. A well-dressed man and woman sat on the bench in front. We waved at them, and they slowed to a stop. We asked if they could give us a ride to town, and they welcomed us to hop on the back.

Once on board, we inspected the couple more closely. They were dressed as if they were going to church, but it was not Sunday, and from the way they talked, we knew they were not illiterate farmers.

They asked about our families and our reason for being on the road. We supplied our usual answers, and then told them we were hungry and had nowhere to sleep that night. It was getting dark. We were beginning to worry about where we would stay.

"That is no problem at all. You will stay with us," the woman responded. "We are Mr. and Mrs. Stanislav, and we have two sons, Jan and Franik. They will be very happy to have boys their own age to play with. We have plenty of room for you."

We could not believe our ears! When we reached the house, two slight boys ran out to greet their parents. They were excited when they found two boys close to their own ages sitting in the wagon.

"Olek, Marjan, this is Jan and Franik, our sons," their boys' mother said. The boys stuck out their hands and Olek and I shook them energetically. Then, while their mother made dinner, the boys gave us a tour of their home. They showed us their bedrooms and the books they studied in school.

When it was time for dinner, the boys' mother asked us to wash our hands, and their father recited a passionate prayer. He asked G-d to bless his family and to bring peace to the world. Then he prayed for our safety as we searched for our families. His prayer was eloquent, and he spoke from the heart. It was not the usual prayer of an ordinary farmer. This man was an educated person.

I looked around. The house, the furniture, the pictures on the wall, the way these people dressed and talked was unlike anything I had encountered before. I didn't ask a single question, and the family volunteered no explanation of who they were or what they did.

The evening's conversation revolved around Olek and me. The boys' father asked about our families, our siblings, our schools, and our fathers' occupations. Of course, they also wanted to know how we had survived the past three years.

My shy friend, Olek, barely said a word: I gave all the answers. Of course, I never mentioned we were Jewish, but I wondered if all the questions would lead to that one. Would he come right out and ask our religion? He knew we had Polish names, and I still wore the cross the priest had given me years before, but he might still be suspicious. I waited, ready to tell him we were Catholic, but he never asked.

After dinner, he prayed again, thanking G-d for the food and the opportunity to meet us. I chimed in, thanking G-d for their kindness, hospitality, and the delicious meal.

After dinner, the boys' mother asked them to help us get ready for the night. The boys each had his own room, so she asked them to move in together for the night so Olek and I could share the other room. The room was small, but to us, it was luxurious. There was a small bed, a dresser, and a few books. The boys' father filled a couple of bags with straw to sleep on, and we all went to bed.

Olek and I crawled into our beds, but could not sleep for another night. We were too excited about our new circumstances. We were curious and wondered about this family. They owned some animals: We had seen two horses, two cows, goats, chickens, and a dog, but they were definitely not ordinary farmers. Most Polish farmers were uneducated because there were no schools in the villages. If they received any education, it came from the local priest who taught the children lessons in Catholic catechism. We puzzled and puzzled over this, until we finally fell asleep as the sun began to rise.

The boys woke us with a call to breakfast. After we ate, the boys gathered their books for school, and Olek and I gathered our bundles for the day's walk. However, before we could leave, it began to snow.

"No school today!" Mr. Stanislav said. "And you boys," he pointed at me and Olek, "you are not going anywhere until the weather improves. Tomorrow, you will go with our sons to school. I'm sure you missed most of your lessons during the war."

Our mouths fell open. Olek and I were so surprised, that we could not utter a single word. Here was a man who had known us less then twenty-four hours, and yet he talked as if we were his own sons.

Olek and I did not object. After the war ended, the roads were dangerous even in good weather. So, instead of heading down the road, we went out to the barn to feed the animals. When we returned, we joined Jan, Franik, and their father as they read a Bible passage and studied the commentary. After that, all four of us were excused to play dominoes until lunch.

We passed the afternoon in much the same way we had spent the morning. That evening, before we enjoyed another delicious dinner, the boys' father recited another long prayer. Then we sat around the table, talking about this and that for a couple of hours before it was time for bed.

On the way to bed, I passed an ornate grandfather's clock. This was the only clock I had seen during the war. Its pleasant ticking and regular chimes were comforting. It was reassuring to know the time of day, to have regular meals and a safe, warm place to sleep. At the end of one day with this family, I felt a sense of predictability and normalcy that I had missed for years. For just a moment, I remembered what a family felt like.

Olek and I fell asleep easily that night. In the morning, the weather was only slightly better, and certainly not good enough for us to travel a long distance on foot. Instead, after feeding the animals, we helped the boys harness the horses to the wagon. The boys' father took the reins, and off we went.

An hour passed before we reached a village centered around a small Catholic church. Inside, the parish priest was waiting. The boys' father introduced us. He told the priest that Olek and I would join the school until the weather improved.

"What will you do then?" the priest asked us with a kind smile. We explained we would go to Warsaw to look for relatives who might have survived the war. The priest seemed moved by our situation. He patted our shoulders and expressed his sympathy. "Well, in the meantime, come with me, and we will see if we can learn a little," he said.

We followed the priest to the chapel where we joined other boys from the village. We studied the Bible and practiced reading. Later that afternoon, the boys' father returned. He took over as teacher so the priest could take care of other business for the church. That was how we learned that our benefactor was a schoolteacher.

The weather failed to improve for several weeks, and Olek and I were in no hurry. As long as the snow and freezing weather continued, we knew we could stay. As days, and then weeks went by, we grew to feel as if this family were our own. We joined the boys at school every day, and we played dominoes together in the evenings. We studied the Bible and took care of the animals in the barn. We felt safe, warm, and even loved.

The boys' parents were very worried about the wounds on my hand and on Olek's foot. We had jagged scars, and where the tissue had contracted, my hand and Olek's foot had contracted as well. One day, they loaded us into the wagon and took us to see a doctor in a nearby village. He examined our wounds carefully, but determined it was too late to do anything to help us.

The weather improved gradually, and as the days grew brighter, our hearts grew heavier, for Olek and I knew the time was coming when we would need to leave. Our hearts were in pieces at the thought of separating from this family. The boys' parents treated us as if we were their own children, and we had come to love them and their sons. We wanted to look for our relatives, but we hated to leave these loving people and this warm, safe home.

The priest who was our teacher pitied us for losing our families at such a young age. He was kind and called us his children. "Boys, you are welcome to stay here as long as you want," he told us again and again. "The Nazis bombed Warsaw day and night before the war was over. It is very dangerous there now. Who knows if there is anyone left for you to find? Perhaps it would be better to start over and let the past go."

We wrestled with the difficult decision of what to do, but we finally decided we had to move on. We still hoped that one of our family members might have survived.

On our last day at the school, we told the priest that, weather permitting; we would leave for Warsaw the next day. He frowned and his brows furrowed. "I understand your longing," Father said, "but I do worry about you. I will pray that you find someone. May you reach your destination safely, and may G-d's angels be with you every hour of the day."

Jan and Franik overheard our conversation with the priest. They approached us in the churchyard, their chins quivering, tears in their eyes. "We heard what you said to Father. Why are you leaving? Did we do something wrong?" they asked.

Olek and I shook our heads. "We hate to leave you. We will miss you terribly," we assured them. "You are like brothers to us, but we can't wait any longer. We have to search for our families. Who knows where they may be? They could be looking for us."

"But you have a family here," they cried. "Don't you like *this* family?"

"Of course, we like you very much. We love you all. But we hope our mothers and fathers are out there somewhere. We must look for them, for who knows what has happened to them?"

By this time, all four of us were crying. How could we leave this family who had taken us in without question, who had loved us and treated us as their own?

Knowing we could easily stay forever made our decision to leave even more difficult. It was heartbreaking to leave a loving family to search for parents and siblings who had probably perished years before; but as long as there was the slightest hope they could be alive, we knew we had to go.

When we got home from school that day, the boys rushed to their mother in the kitchen and told her we were leaving. By the time we entered the house, the boys were hugging their mother, crying. Mrs. Stanislav patted their backs, holding back her own tears. "Why are they leaving, Mommy?" they cried. "We thought they were our friends."

She hugged her sons, but she gazed at me and Olek. "I also wish they didn't have to leave," she said, looking at us lovingly, "but they need to find out about their families. If they don't go, they could live the rest of their lives wondering about their parents, sisters, and brothers." She hugged her sons closer. "Imagine if you were in their shoes. It is not that they don't love us, children. This is something they *have* to do."

That evening, the boys' mother made a special dinner, and her husband prayed for a long time. He thanked G-d for blessing his family, then asked Him to guide and protect us on our journey. When he finished his prayer, we ate in silence. The atmosphere was heavy, filled with anticipation of the next day's departure. After dinner, we played dominoes with the boys, but instead of the laughter that usually accompanied our games, we played quietly and shook hands before going to bed.

There was no way to sleep that night. Olek and I cried over the pain and sadness we were causing this family. We wept for the loss we felt and knew we would continue to feel in the days and weeks ahead. We reconsidered our decision many times, but always with the same conclusion. Of all the sleepless nights we had experienced since the labor camp, this was the longest. We were still awake when the sun came up.

When the family finally awoke, we prayed and ate breakfast together, then said goodbye before the boys left for school with their father. For Olek and I, the sorrow was overwhelming, perhaps because we had never had the chance to say goodbye to our own families. We stood in the cold spring air, sacks of food and a few extra clothes hanging from our shoulders. The goodbyes we had never said to our own parents and siblings mingled with the sorrow we felt at leaving this family we had grown to love. For a few final moments, we clung to these warm-hearted people, choking back our sobs. We hugged one another, and promised we would never forget each other.

Olek and I walked down the road in silence, choking back our tears, lost in our private thoughts. The war had been over for months. We no longer had to worry about encountering German soldiers, but we still faced the challenge of finding food, water, and shelter every day. Although it was early spring, the ground was still frozen. We would freeze if we slept outside, and no crops grew alongside the road. Our survival depended on our luck and the kindness of strangers once again.

CHAPTER 26
RETRACING STEPS BACK TO WARSAW

Toward afternoon, Olek and I came to a rest area where farmers could feed their horses and buy something to eat on their way to and from the market. We walked from farmer to farmer, asking for food and shelter in return for work on their farms. Some of the farmers gave us food, but it was shelter for the night that we really needed. Toward the end of the day, we found a farmer who took us home and let us stay the night.

We rode on the farmer's wagon for several hours until we arrived at a small village. His home was tiny—one small room. There was no running water or electricity, just a well outside, a wood stove, and a kerosene lamp. The farmer's wife was old and sickly, but she was very friendly and kind. She said they had no children, and she cried when she heard that we had lost our families during the war.

Later that evening, she prepared a delicious meal, and we ate our fill. Over dinner, we discussed where Olek and I would sleep. The house was tiny, and they apologized that we would have to sleep in the barn. We assured them that we would be comfortable with the horse and cow. They helped us make a bed of hay, and they provided us with blankets. We slept very well near the warmth of the animals and their slow, regular breathing.

The farmer woke us when he came to feed his animals in the morning. We washed, ate breakfast, and prepared to get on our way. As always, we thanked the farmer and his wife for their kindness and asked G-d to bless them.

We had turned to leave when the farmer's wife stood up and commanded, "Wait!" The Germans were gone, but anti-Semitism still raged among the Poles. Perhaps they suspected we were Jewish. Our fear of being discovered and punished for our religion was always present.

My heart hammered in my chest until it hurt to breathe. What if I have a heart attack, I wondered? In the following second, I envisioned myself in the hospital. They would call the police and Olek and I would be shot for pretending to be Christians. We heard of stories like this over and over during the war. Perhaps the Germans were still waiting for us somewhere.

The farmer's wife asked her husband a question, but the sound of my heartbeat was so loud, I had trouble hearing what she said. I could only hear his answer.

"Of course you can stay a few more days. Then we will take you with us when we go to market in Warsaw," he said. "It will be much better than walking such a long way in this cold weather."

My mind went blank as I struggled to understand what I was hearing. They were not turning us in? They were asking us to stay longer? They were offering to take us all the way to Warsaw? I couldn't believe it. Where had I lost the hope that helped me to survive the war? I felt ashamed at my lack of faith in G-d's protection.

We agreed to stay on for a few more days until the couple left for Warsaw, but as the week crept by, we began to feel trapped in their tiny, dark house. We had nothing to do but feed the animals and wait for time to pass. It was too early in the spring to work in the field, so we sat at the table while the farmer read the Bible, his wife sewed, and the hours ticked by.

The night before we left for Warsaw, we reviewed the plans for our trip. The farmer announced we would leave after breakfast, then travel by wagon for six or seven hours to a village that was still quite a ways from Warsaw.

"There is one problem, boys," the farmer said. "My wife and I have decided to stay with friends in the village for a few days. We will arrive after dark, and we aren't sure if there will be a place for you to sleep."

Olek and I were concerned and frustrated. How would we find a place to sleep in a strange town after dark? Now, after a week of waiting, we would be no closer to Warsaw than when we started. Our only choice was to go along and hope for the best. We fell asleep that night worrying and praying about what would happen the following night.

We left after breakfast the next day. We stopped at noon to rest the horses and the farmer gave us something to eat. When it was nearly dark, we arrived at the home of the farmer's friends. They were friendly people, clearly happy to see the farmer and his wife; however, their home was small and, as we feared, there was no place for us to sleep.

The farmer's friend told us there was a place nearby where we could stay. He offered to take us there himself, and we gratefully accepted his offer. Within minutes, he had hitched his wagon, and we set out.

Along the way, he explained that when the war ended, there were thousands of survivors traveling through European villages and town. Like Olek and me, these people were returning from the war, from the partisans, from forced labor and concentration camps. Many were homeless, their houses destroyed, their families lost or killed. Others were simply passing through, walking back from wherever the war had left them when it ended. To accommodate these travelers, some towns opened shelters where survivors could sleep and eat a free meal before continuing on their journey. The farmer's friend took us to such a place and introduced us to the person in charge.

"You will be safe here. Good luck in your search," he said, and then he left. We never saw him again.

That night, we were well fed and took the first hot showers we'd had in days. We shared a bunk bed in a large room where other war survivors also slept.

At breakfast the next morning, we learned that it would take two or three more days to walk to Warsaw, so we decided to leave immediately. We thanked the people who ran the house and headed out. We hoped to hitch a ride with a farmer on his way to the city, but by noon we still walked at the side of the road, tired and chilled to the bone. We tried to dig potatoes for our lunch, but the fields were still frozen. We walked on, with only our faith and hope to keep us warm.

At dusk, a horse and wagon approached. We signaled the driver to stop and were surprised and thankful when he did. We looked up at the old man, explained our situation, and asked if he could give us food or shelter for the night. He told us his wife was sickly, but said we could sleep in his barn. We thanked G-d, believing He had heard our prayers.

When we arrived at the old man's house, his wife greeted us in the traditional Polish fashion and invited us into the house. Her skin was worn and wrinkled, and her back was bent and painfully twisted from years of labor. She placed bread, butter, and milk on the table and invited us to eat. "This is just a snack," she said. "We will have dinner in an hour." The bread and butter were fresh, and we had not tasted milk in many days. It was delicious.

The evening passed, as so many had before, with questions about our families, with prayers, and with Bible study into the night. Again, we slept in the barn, keeping warm with the horse and cow. We went on our way as soon as the sun came up.

At noon, we ate the loaf of bread the couple had given us before we left. Our mouths were parched without anything to drink, so when we heard the sound of running water, we left the road and found a small stream. We drank until we were full, then began to walk again until it began to grow dark. There were no villages or houses anywhere, and we worried about the cold, rainy night ahead.

A few kilometers away, we saw a tiny spark of light. The distance did not seem far, but we walked a long time before we reached a small village of four houses. We knocked on the first door. The man who answered was shocked to see two bedraggled boys standing on his doorstep.

"In the name of G-d, what are you boys doing here so late?" he said. "We are twenty kilometers from the closest town—how did you get here?"

He invited us in, and we told him our story. It was long past the dinner hour, but his wife cooked some eggs. While we ate, we told the couple how we had survived the war. We told them that our faith in G-d had led us this far and protected us from harm. We told about the farms where we had worked, and the families who had taken pity on us. We talked and talked, and they listened intently. Two things we never mentioned that night: fighting in the Ghetto or with the partisans. We were unsure how they would feel about Jews or partisans, and we dared not take the risk.

As always, before we ate, and after we finished, we recited the Catholic prayers we knew so well, and asked the Almighty to bless these kind people.

The couple began to worry about where we would sleep in their tiny home. They were shocked when we volunteered to sleep in the barn. "We have slept in people's barns many times," I assured them.

"You have slept in the barns with animals?" the woman said, her eyebrows raised in surprise.

"Yes, many times," I repeated. "It is warm, and we are happy for the shelter."

The next day, we walked until it was nearly dark again. In the distance we saw a large house with bright lights, which we knew must be electricity. As we got closer, we recognized it was a roadhouse.

Trucks, horses and wagons waited outside. Inside, the owners and drivers gathered to eat, drink, and exchange stories.

We entered the roadhouse and watched a chubby, red-faced woman serving food from behind a counter. Olek was hesitant, but I approached the counter and asked the woman for food and lodging. She told us to sit at a table, and without asking anything, she placed food before us. "Eat, my children!" she said.

When we finished, she asked all the questions we had grown to expect, and we answered as we always did. The woman was silent for a while, and we saw sadness in her eyes.

"Perhaps you have heard this before," she said, "but Warsaw is in ruins; most of the buildings were destroyed by bombs and fire. First, the Jews fought the Germans in the Ghetto. So, the Nazis burned it to the ground. I don't think there is even one building left, and there is certainly no one living there anymore. Then, in 1944, the Polish resistance organized an uprising. That's when the Germans bombed the rest of Warsaw."

We had seen the destruction of the Ghetto, and had heard rumors about the rest of the city, but we had hoped that somehow the rumors were wrong and the city would be there when we returned. We had dreamed of walking into familiar neighborhoods, reuniting with family members who had simply been away at work camp. Now, our spirits fell.

"We appreciate the warning," I said, "but we have to go anyway. Can you tell us how far it is to the next town?"

"Grojec is just 20 kilometers from here," she said.

I was surprised to find we were so close to the town where the police chief had given me the fake birth certificate with a Polish name. Grojec was where I had received the key to my survival. I was anxious to go. I hoped I could find the policeman and thank him for the papers that I still carried with me.

"Olek, we must go to Grojec tomorrow, but it is too late tonight," I said. Then I turned to the waitress, "Do you think we can stay here until daybreak?"

"We are open all night, so make yourselves comfortable," she answered. "I am going to ask one of these farmers to give you a ride into town in the morning when he goes to market."

Olek and I looked around the room and found a bench in the corner. We leaned against the wall and nodded off for a couple of hours. Sometime past midnight, the woman woke us and introduced us to a farmer who agreed to give us a ride to town. His wagon was loaded with sacks of potatoes. Olek, still weaker than me, sat on the bench in the front of the wagon. I balanced on a sack of potatoes in back.

The farmer's horse was very small. He could barely pull the heavy wagon. He plodded along, and when we came to a hill, we all jumped off and pushed the wagon to the top. Then, we let the horse rest before going on our way again. We could have probably walked to Grojec more quickly, but at least we had time to rest, and with Olek's injured foot, it was a blessing to ride even if the road was bumpy and full of potholes.

We arrived in Grojec at sunrise, and the farmer found a good spot at the market. We fed and watered the horse, and unloaded the potatoes while we waited for the town offices to open.

At daybreak, we left the market and wandered into the center of town. Grojec was silent, and the streets were empty. The burned-out shells of ruined buildings rose from the rubble of the streets. If I hadn't known for sure, I never would have believed it was the same town I had visited three years before when I became Marian Redlicki.

We finally found the town hall—just two small rooms in a tiny house. We introduced ourselves to the couple that worked there and told them our story. We asked if they could help us to find food and shelter in Grojec.

The man asked for my birth certificate and I handed him my faded, crumpled document—the very one I had received there just three years before.

"So, you are Marian Redlicki?" he asked.

"Yes, sir."

"And you," he said to Olek, "do you have a birth certificate?"

Olek handed him his documents and said, "I am Olek Polanski."

I looked over at Olek's familiar face. We had been through so much together. We had shared our fears, our hiding places, our hopes and sorrows, but we had never told one another our Jewish names. We were so deeply committed to our false identities that we had never even whispered our true names to one another.

After the official checked our documents, he said, "Grojec is a small town and we don't have many resources to help you. But if you want to find out if one of your relatives is alive in Warsaw, we will try to help you get there."

He took out a scrap of paper and wrote an address. "This place will give you food for the day and a place to sleep tonight. Come back tomorrow morning."

We thanked him and headed to the address he gave us. There, we found a hotel of sorts. The proprietor and his wife acted as if they were expecting us. They welcomed us with warm smiles and a hot breakfast.

After our meal, I tried to find the chief of police so I could thank him and let him know I had survived the war. I wandered through the streets, but nothing looked familiar, and I could not find his sister's street.

In the afternoon, we returned to the market and helped the farmer load his truck. We told him we had found a place to stay, and we thanked him for his help. We asked G-d to protect him and his family. Then we returned to the hotel that would shelter us for the night.

CHAPTER 27

SEARCHING THE LISTS OF SURVIVORS

The hotel was filled with travelers going to Warsaw to find relatives they had lost in the war. If they were Jewish, they never said so, and neither did we. We were fed a hot dinner, and we slept on real beds. Olek and I shared a bunk bed on one side of the room, Olek in the bottom bunk because he was afraid of heights. Two other boys shared a bunk on the other side of the room. The four of us talked for many hours that night, sharing stories of our families and our experiences during the war. We finally said goodnight and fell asleep.

In the morning, we had an early breakfast and then boarded the small bus that would take ten of us from Grojec to Tarczyn. The bus was old and dilapidated, a relic from the war. It inched along slowly and, after an hour, it overheated and quit entirely. The driver left us in the bus while he went to find water for the radiator. When he returned, we started our journey again, but made frequent stops to prevent the bus from overheating.

Approaching Tarczyn, I felt melancholy at retracing the steps I had taken almost three years before. I had fled to Tarczyn on the night I first escaped the Ghetto. I had been just a child, though I thought of myself as a man. Now, here I was, years later, having seen and experienced so much, returning to the place where my journey began.

The driver stopped the bus at city hall. "I can't continue to Warsaw with Jews," he called after us as we got off the bus. I looked back, surprised at his comment. Although Olek and I had never said anything about being Jewish, apparently others in our group had. I wondered whether it was a law or personal prejudice that barred him from transporting Jews into the city.

Tarczyn was a small town that had been home to a Jewish community that manufactured leather goods, especially shoes, before the war. When I got off the bus that day, I could not believe my eyes. The town was nearly gone. Most of it had been destroyed by the war, and there was no sign of the busy factories or commercial centers that had once made this a bustling business center. Now, only a few stores were in business.

We walked to the town hall, where a young clerk welcomed us. "How can I help you?" the clerk said. Our group asked for food and transportation to Warsaw. "I can help you find food, but there is only one person who transports people to Warsaw. He has a covered truck and he goes twice a week, but we have nothing to do with that here."

Without a word, he turned and left the room and was gone for quite a while. We thought he had forgotten us when he returned and said, "Okay, the truck will take you all to Warsaw in the morning. For tonight, you will have to split up and sleep with five different families. Two of you can stay together if you wish."

Olek and I stayed overnight with a nice, older couple. Their son had left home to find work in the city, because there were no jobs in Tarczyn, so they let us stay in his room where we shared an old straw mattress and a single blanket. They apologized for the meager accommodations, but we assured them it was far better than sleeping in a barn with horses and cows.

In the morning, we returned to the city hall and found an old, flatbed truck waiting to transport us to Warsaw. A wood-burning stove hung off one side of the truck. The stove heated water to power the truck's steam engine. The driver's helper fueled the stove with wood from the back of the truck to keep it running.

When he was ready to go, the driver approached our group. "Okay, everyone, climb aboard," he said.

The nine of us studied the truck. The cab was enclosed, but the back, where he indicated we would ride, had no sides.

"That doesn't look safe," said one of the potential passengers. "If you hit a pothole, we will bounce right off." Others agreed, but the driver told them not to worry. He guided three men onto the truck bed and asked them to sit with their backs to the cabin, three across. He guided a second set of three people to sit between the legs of the first three. Finally, a third group of three, including me, sat between the legs of the second. Once we were situated, the driver looped a rope across our laps, and tied us to the truck.

"There," he announced, "you're all set." With a satisfied smile, he hopped into the cab and started the engine.

The truck rattled down the road toward Warsaw, and we held on in back, stacked and strapped like firewood. When the truck jolted into a pothole, everyone groaned, though it was most uncomfortable for those at the bottom of the heap. When we rounded a corner, we all hoped the ropes would hold. The old steam engine sputtered and coughed, but we finally reached city hall in the afternoon. The driver unloaded us and quickly drove away.

Officials called each one of us into a separate room and interrogated us, asking the same questions over and over. When they were satisfied with our answers, we were all transported again, this time by covered truck, across the Visla River to Praga, where the Jewish Committee was located. There, we answered more questions. The officials told us we would have to wait for about a week for our appointments with the Committee, after which we would be free to go elsewhere.

Olek and I were invited to stay at a large house where we met other boys, and a few girls, about our age who were also homeless because of the war. A motherly, middle-aged woman was in charge of the house, and a younger girl helped her. She had survived the war because her blonde hair and blue eyes allowed her to pass as a Gentile in the Aryan part of Warsaw. She led us to the dining room for dinner, and then took us back to the headquarters of the Jewish Committee.

The walls of the Jewish Committee headquarters were completely covered with white pieces of paper that fluttered in the breeze every time the door opened or closed. The main room was filled with Jews who stood, staring at the papers on the walls.

"What are all those papers?" we asked our blonde-haired friend.

"Those are the lists," she said, "the lists of survivors."

She went on to explain that hundreds of thousands of Jews had been left homeless and impoverished by the war. Across Europe, Jewish survivors reported to displaced person camps, where their names and information was collected and shared with other centers in other cities in hopes that families and friends could reunite. The papers listed the names, ages and birthplaces of these Jews. The only way to find someone was to search the lists, one name at a time. The headquarters building always overflowed with Jews who scoured the lists night and day.

When Olek and I saw the endless lists of names posted on the walls of the huge room, we knew that we would surely find a relative or friend somewhere. My heart raced with hope and I began to search the papers, expecting at any moment to find the name of my mother or father, my sister or brother. I couldn't wait to be reunited, to see my family again. I couldn't wait to find out where they had been, to see their smiles and feel their hugs. I wanted to tell my parents about my struggles and have them reassure me that those days were now past.

Olek and I read the lists tirelessly. As the days went by, our search became wearisome and discouraging. Most people gave up after a few short days. Olek and I read the lists for five days before we began to lose hope.

We stayed in the big house all that week, waiting for our appointments with the Jewish Committee. When our turns came, they interviewed each of us separately, asking very detailed questions about our families and how we had survived. I told them my entire story—the true story—of how I had escaped the Ghetto. I told them I had been given a false birth certificate, had hidden on farms, had been imprisoned and escaped from a labor camp, had fought in the Ghetto Uprising and, later, with the partisans. I told them my real name, Menachem Taiblum, my father's name, Israel, and my mother's name Rosa. I told them I was born in 1929 and had lived at 53 Panska Street.

My interviewer watched me closely and wrote down everything I said. When I was done talking, he told me to return the next day to find out what would happen next.

That afternoon, Olek and I wandered up and down the streets of Warsaw, trying to find something that looked familiar, but the buildings had been bombed and burned, and the Ghetto was demolished. It was a pile of rubble, and nothing looked the same.

The next morning, the dining room in the big house was crowded with young boys and older teenagers waiting for breakfast. Olek and I knew no one. We ate, then packed the few things we owned. Twenty of us went back to meet with the clerk at the Jewish Committee office.

The clerk asked Olek and me the same questions he had asked the day before. When he was finally satisfied that we were telling the truth, he handed each of us a card on which our names were written. Olek and I still used our fictitious names of Marjan Redlicki and Olek Polanski because those were the names on our only identification papers. The cards entitled us to free meals at any restaurant and free lodging at any motel in Poland, at the expense of the Polish government. They were good for two years.

The clerk suggested how to begin searching for our relatives. He wished us luck, but did not look very hopeful. We thanked him and left the building.

"Olek, where do you think we should go next?" I asked.

Olek was silent. I thought perhaps he had not heard me, so I repeated the question. "Where shall we go, Olek?" More silence.

Olek was looking away, his face tilted down so I could not see his expression. "Olek?" I asked. "Are you alright?"

He rubbed at his eye with the back of one hand. "What is it, Olek? What's the matter?" I asked.

"Marjan, it's time for me to go back to my home town," he said.

My heart sank. I knew this day would come, that Olek would need to go his own way at some point, but I had dreaded it. I couldn't speak.

"If anyone in my family survived, they will be there, not here in Warsaw." I knew he was right, but I could not face the thought of being alone, without my only friend. We had been constant companions since 1942. We had taken care of one another, comforted each other, nursed each other's injuries. We had fought together, laughed together, nearly died together. We had grown closer than brothers. I loved Olek dearly, and I knew that when we parted, we would probably lose one another in the post-war chaos and never see each other again.

"You are sure this is the right time to go?" I asked quietly. He nodded his head and shot me a quick, tearful glance.

"I hope you find someone, Olek," I said. "I hope your parents survived."

"I hope the same for you, my friend," he answered.

"I will never forget you, Olek," I said.

"Nor I you," he replied. At this point, tears covered our cheeks as we embraced one another. Neither of us dared to say another word for fear of crying out loud. So, without another word, Olek turned and walked away. I watched as he disappeared around a corner. I never saw him again.

Parting with my friend was one of the most painful separations I have ever experienced. For years, I searched for him, but because I did not know him by his Jewish name, my search was always futile. I hope and pray this dear friend from those tender and terrible years has had a safe and happy life.

CHAPTER 28
MEETING A MESSENGER FROM ISRAEL

When I returned to the Jewish Committee office, they told me that the Nazis had focused their murderous efforts on the largest cities and most densely populated Jewish communities. Some Jews could still be found in tiny villages that dotted the countryside. This renewed my hope. I had many relatives who lived outside of Warsaw, working in the leather business. I would start my search in Falenice where my family members owned summer cottages by the lake.

The train to Falenice was scheduled to leave on Friday, so I spent two more days studying the list of displaced persons and slept at the big house with the other young survivors.

On Friday morning, I got to the train station before the train arrived. I was hungry, so I used the card from the Jewish Committee and bought a sandwich. Minutes later, I heard a train whistle screech through the still morning air, and the train puffed up the tracks. As soon as I boarded, the train chugged off at a painfully slow speed. It took all day to travel the 40 kilometers to Falencia. When I arrived, I ran through the deserted streets, and got to the city hall just before it closed. The elderly clerk looked surprised to see a young teenager enter alone.

"Can I help you?" he asked. When I showed him the card from the Jewish Committee, he looked even more startled.

"I have never seen a card like this," he said. He paused and read aloud from the back: "The holder of this card should be given any help necessary." He thought for a moment before asking, "What kind of help do you want?"

"I need a place to eat and a place to stay tonight," I said. He directed me to the only hotel in town.

I stopped along the way for dinner, and although the restaurant's patrons stared at me, I was served something to eat. In fact, the manager invited me to return there for dinner every night I was in town.

After dinner, I walked in the direction of the hotel. The moon cast ghostly shadows through the ruins of buildings that had been destroyed by the war. There was no sign of the Jewish community I remembered. The pretty vacation cottages were gone and the streets seemed dark and foreboding. I ran as quickly as I could to a dilapidated, one-story house. This was the only hotel in what was once a busy and lovely vacation village.

There appeared to be no one on duty when I entered the hotel. A bell sat on the reception desk, so I rang it. Some minutes later, a door opened behind the reception area, and an old man came out. He glared at me.

"What do you want?" he barked. I told him I needed a place to sleep for one night, and that I would leave for Otwock in the morning.

"What are you doing here?" he asked. As always, I answered that I was looking for relatives who might have survived the war.

"Have any money?" he asked. I pulled the card from my pocket and handed it to him. He flipped it back and forth in his hand, read it, and returned it to me. "Come with me. I'll show you where you can sleep," he said.

I followed him to a small room, furnished with a single bed, a table and chair, and a radio. The shower and washroom were down the hall. I was tired from a long day of traveling, and I was chilled from my walk across town looking for recognizable landmarks and any sign of Jewish life. The places my family had once enjoyed stood in ruins. Without Olek, I had no one to talk to, and the locals looked at me with suspicion and distrust. I had hoped to find someone I knew, but I was still alone and feared I might always be. I choked on my disappointment.

In the morning, I used my card to pay the bill, then left for the train station. The passenger car was full, so I sat next to an elderly woman who gave me directions to the City Hall and told me a few things about Otwock.

I reached City Hall by mid-afternoon, and showed my card to the young woman at the reception desk. She went into the back office and brought out a nicely dressed, older man.

"Finding you a place to sleep and something to eat is no problem," he said, "but finding your family may be more difficult. We can get you a list of the Jews who lived in Otwock before the war, and you can look for familiar names."

He gave me a letter that would provide for my hotel room, and the girl said to return to a nearby restaurant in two hours for dinner. She held on to my card and studied me for several minutes. Her eyes seemed to ask what was so special about me that I received free meals and lodging.

I left the building, but did not have the strength to walk anymore. I was exhausted, discouraged, hungry, and lonely. I sat on a bench in a nearby park and waited. When I returned to the restaurant, men dressed in working clothes sat at the tables, eating and talking. They obviously knew each other. The hostess seated me at an empty table in the corner and gave me a glass of water. While I waited for dinner, an older man approached my table and asked if he could join me. "I am Frank," he said, holding out his hand. I shook it and told him my name was Marian.

"What is a young boy like you doing alone in this town?" he asked. I repeated the story I had told so many times before.

Over dinner, the man advised me to start with the list they would give me the next day. "First, look for names you recognize. If you find one, go to the address on the list and check it out. Don't be discouraged, it can take a long time."

I thanked him and left the restaurant feeling a bit more encouraged. I would start my search again in the morning.

The next day, the man at City Hall gave me a list of 30 names and addresses. He wished me luck, and I went on my way. I spent the next three days combing town, visiting every address on the list. I never found one Jewish person. The homes that once housed Jewish families were either destroyed or were now inhabited by non-Jews. All signs of Jewish life had been erased.

I returned to my room every evening feeling melancholy and disappointed. This had once been a vibrant Jewish community, full of life, families, and culture. Now it was gone—swallowed without trace.

On the fourth day, I gave up and moved on. I headed in the direction of Bialystok, a large city not far from the Russian border. I thought perhaps Bialystok was far enough from Germany that the Nazis had not reached it. I hoped I would find a thriving Jewish community there. I would give anything to hear Jewish music and to celebrate in the traditions of my family. The longer I thought about it, the more certain I became that, because this city was far from Warsaw, I would surely find someone I knew.

Bialystock was quite a long trip from Otwock, so on the way there, I stopped at as many towns as possible, always hoping to find someone. Sadly, I was disappointed at every stop.

One of the towns I visited was Mezericze, a town where many Jewish-owned industries had flourished before the war. Here, Jewish workers had manufactured clothing, leather goods, and household items. As in other towns, the clerk at city hall provided me with a list of possible Jewish residents. I quickly scanned the list, and my uncle's name nearly jumped off the page. My heart raced. Perhaps I would find my mother's brother and be reunited with my cousins—maybe even with my own parents. Anticipation and hope swelled in my heart. Breathless, I ran to the address on the list. I walked up the steps and knocked on the door, choking back tears of hope.

An elderly woman opened the door. I had never seen her before. We were definitely not related. She glared at me. "What do you want?" she asked with an unfriendly tone.

I smiled at her, hoping to melt some of her indifference. "My name is Menachem Taiblum. I'm looking for my uncle. He used to live in this house," I said.

The woman's disgusted look contorted into a sneer. She raised her hands toward the sky. "Oh my G-d! Oh my G-d! Are Jews still alive?" she cried. "I thought Hitler had finished them off! I thought Poland was *judenrein* (clean of Jews)."

Her words struck me like a blow, and I reeled backward. I couldn't take my eyes off her angry face. Fire burned inside my head, and my heart began to race. My throat grew tight and I knew I was about to cry. I was determined not to give her that satisfaction, so without a word, I turned and walked away. I staggered down the street, my hope of finding anyone I used to know or love vanishing with every step.

After everything that had happened—the pain, the suffering, the death, the loss—hatred was still alive and well. Where anti-Semitism had grown, it would remain forever, I thought. Nothing would ever change.

I fell into a state of complete despair. Ever since the night I had returned to the Ghetto and found my family missing, I had clung to the hope of someday finding them. They were good people, innocent people. Why would G-d have allowed the Nazis to hurt them? They had to be alive—somewhere. That hope had sustained me during the war and the difficult months that followed. Now, that hope was dying a slow and painful death. My heart broke over and over. I would never find my family. I would never find my sister or brother. They were gone. Dead. I had to accept it.

I was done searching. I told myself it was pointless to look anymore. I abandoned my journey to Bialystok. What was the point of going? How long was I supposed to continue searching, just to be disappointed time and again? I decided to return to Warsaw.

At the station, I discovered the train to Warsaw would not arrive for two days. All I could think of was getting away from this wretched town. For the next 48 hours, I walked up and down the streets of Mezericze, trying to silence the voice that played over and over in my head. As much as I tried, I could not forget that woman's sour face or her harsh words: "Are Jews still alive? Are Jews still alive?" It was like a nightmare without end.

I couldn't sleep at night, and I lay awake wondering how it was possible that, after the greatest tragedy that had befallen humanity, there were still people in the world like that woman. Nothing would ever change.

On Friday morning, I left for Radom, a large city near Warsaw. As usual, I headed toward the city hall, running through war-ravaged streets to get there before it closed. Nearly every building had been demolished by bombs and stood abandoned, crumbling, and burned. Only on the outskirts of town did I see a few businesses struggling to survive.

The people at city hall helped me to find housing and food. The next morning, I caught the first train for the seven-hour trip to Warsaw. We passed through many small towns and stopped a time or two, so we could find something to eat. At one stop, an older man boarded the train and sat next to me. He identified the ruins of one building after another as we headed into Warsaw.

Once within the city limits, I took a bus toward Praga and headed to the Jewish Committee headquarters. After seeing so many ruins,

I was surprised and relieved to find it was still there. Two years had passed since the war had ended, but Jewish survivors still trickled into Warsaw every day, trying to locate family members. Day after day, they still poured over the lists of displaced persons that lined the walls. I looked around, but I did not recognize anyone.

Many Poles still hated Jews and there was often violence toward Jews in Warsaw. That evening, a Committee representative explained which streets and houses in Warsaw were safe for us, and warned us to stay in at night and to travel together. He assigned everyone a place to sleep somewhere in the city and told us to pair up for safety before leaving. Most people joined someone they already knew, but since Olek had left, I was alone. I was relieved when a young man, just a few years older than me, asked if I would like to room with him. Over the following days, we got to know each other and walked around Warsaw together. We stopped at Committee headquarters every day to see if new names had been added to the list of survivors on the wall. None of the names were familiar to me, and neither were the faces that studied them.

We spent several weeks floating in an unsettled, pointless existence. I had given up hope and was growing restless with the waiting and searching. My friend and I spent hours discussing what to do with our lives. It seemed that Europe was still hostile toward Jews, and I did not want to stay where my family had obviously been killed, but I did not know where else to go. I considered Australia because I heard they were friendly to Jews and would take in any Jewish survivor without question. I considered South America, the United States, and Canada.

Then one day, I met a man from Israel, and my decision became easy. The man introduced himself as a *sheliach*, a messenger from the government of Israel. He had come to Europe to recruit new immigrants. He invited us to move to Israel where all Jews, especially war survivors, would have a home.

Within a few days, he had recruited a group of young people, including me. We travelled by bus to the train station where he bought us tickets for the 12-hour ride to the town of Klocko near the Czech border. He took us to a large house owned by the Jewish Committee and we lived there while we waited for enough people to fill a ship to Israel.

While waiting in Klocko, I made friends with a couple whose younger brother had been killed in the war. They treated me well and said that I could fill his place in their family. I spent all of my free time with them.

One night, without warning, we were told that we would leave for Israel the following day. After breakfast, a military truck covered with canvas waited in the street outside the big house. I was in the first of two groups that boarded the truck, carrying my few belongings. Women and young boys sat on benches around the perimeter, and men sat on the floor or perched on their suitcases. The second group watched as we rode off, our organizers promising that they would return to get them soon.

We rode for several hours. When we arrived at the Czech border, the guards came out and met with our representative from the Jewish Committee. Within minutes, the gate at the border crossing began to open. We were on our way!

Seconds before we crossed through the gate, a military jeep with four Russian soldiers cut in front of our truck. An officer stepped out of the jeep and announced, "We have received reliable notice that there are speculators on this bus, carrying a lot of American money. The truck must go back to Klocko so we can investigate this."

Looking around me in the dim light of our truck, I saw shock and exhaustion on the faces of my fellow Jews. I was certain no one in our group had a single dollar. I was sure that most of these people, including me, did not even know the color of an American dollar bill. This was a discouraging turn of events, but most of us were so accustomed to things going wrong, that we simply resigned ourselves to deal with whatever came next.

The truck turned back to Klocko, and the soldiers led us straight to the city jail. They locked us into jail cells, where each person was individually searched. The soldiers tore open our bags and searched our belongings. They cut the lining from our jackets and the heels from our shoes, but they never found an American dollar.

When the search for illegal money proved fruitless, the soldiers changed their accusation. Now they said we were trying to leave the country illegally and would need to remain in jail.

My fellow travelers and I were incarcerated for several days in the dark, cold jail at Klocko until the Jewish Committee succeeded in bribing the right officials to arrange our release. We were freed on condition that we apply for passports before leaving the country. We could not believe the barriers we had to overcome to leave a country that did not even want us.

We returned to the house in Klocko and found more Jews had congregated for the trip to Israel. The man in charge called a meeting shortly after we arrived.

"Our numbers are growing," he said, "and because we don't know how long we will have to wait for passports, we must all contribute to supporting one another. You will need to get a job here in Klocko to help pay for our food and rent."

I thought a job sounded interesting, and I was ready to go out and find work immediately. Not everyone in our group felt the same way. Some people grumbled they couldn't find a job because we were leaving soon. They said it would be impossible to find a job in their chosen profession.

"It doesn't matter what kind of job you get, but you must try," our leader said. He gave us a few tips about where to apply and which areas of town were safest for Jews.

I was restless that night, my mind whirling, trying to imagine where I could find a job in this strange town. I found comfort remembering I had survived the war with faith and hope. I fell asleep, certain G-d would help me find a job sooner or later.

The next day, each of us was given a little book in which to write the names and addresses of businesses we visited each day. The business owners had to sign the book to prove we had asked for work.

Again, many survivors complained: "Why should I get a job when I am preparing to leave the country?" They were satisfied to simply wait, eating, sleeping and walking around town, but the man in charge was firm, "We don't have any idea how long this will take. You must go out and look for a job."

After breakfast, I asked for directions to the Jewish Committee office. There, I explained the situation to the clerk and asked if he knew of a Jewish establishment where I could find work. The clerk was surprised by my request. He had never heard of a situation like ours. An older, nicely dressed man summoned me into his office and provided me with the information I needed.

I took the business of finding a job seriously. At least it gave me something concrete and productive to do. I visited nearly every business on my list. I did not get hired that day, but I didn't let that discourage me. I went back out the next day and got a job as a deliveryman.

Every day, I pulled a hand truck loaded with heavy boxes of red wine up and down the cobblestone streets. I made friends with my fellow workers and with the people to whom I delivered the wine. I had a place to go and a purpose for each day. I was more satisfied than I had been in a long time. I kept the job until the day I received my passport.

When the Germans pulled out of Poland, the Russian Communist party took over. The company I worked for was founded and managed by high-ranking officials in the Communist party. As spring approached that year, I was told that May 1 was International Workers Holiday, the most important holiday of the year for Communists. Our company managers required all workers to attend a public demonstration on May 1. If anyone refused, he or she would be fired.

Under that threat, all of us were naturally present at the May 1 demonstration. The event was attended by every child, worker, policeman, and Communist party leader in town. We heard many speeches praising the virtues of Communism and the Workers Party. A police band played until late at night, and people sang communist songs.

At work the following day, one of the communist managers came to fire anyone who had not attended the rally. My fellow workers and I covered for one another, and no one was identified. We discovered there was an informer among our co-workers who passed along information about those who opposed communism. Once we found out who the spy was, we were careful about what we said around him.

After several months, our passports finally arrived. A sense of relief and excitement filled our hearts, and we prepared to leave. I went to work the next morning and told my supervisor I would leave for Israel the next day.

"Why would you leave a good steady job and go where the economic situation is difficult? It isn't safe there. Your life will be uncertain. You should stay here in Poland—a good, free country," my manager said.

I shook my head and stared at him. The man meant well, but his experience of Poland differed from mine. He had not lost his family, endured hatred and bigotry, and lived with danger and fear. He believed in Poland and in Communism. For him and for many others, Poland was a good country, but for me, Poland was already in my past. In my heart, I had left Poland and all its nightmares long ago.

My supervisor and the other managers convinced a few people from our group to remain in Poland, but the majority of us boarded a train that carried us through Austria and on to Italy. I waited many months in Italy, but eventually, I stood on board a ship bound for Israel and watched the shores of Italy fade into the mist. As Europe disappeared in the distance, a heavy weight began to lift from my shoulders and hope for a bright, new future filled my heart.

POST SCRIPT

I have never discovered the fate of my family—or that of my relatives and friends. Despite my vow to give up, I have always continued to look for their names or any sign that they survived. I have found nothing. It is as if they never existed.

Many years after that chilly August night when my family disappeared, I learned that all Jewish residents of the Little Ghetto were evacuated that week. The Nazis drove the Jews who lived in the area south of Choldna Street into the large Ghetto, where there was no room for them to live. Perhaps, like thousands of others, my family was immediately deported to Treblinka. Perhaps they were among the small group of ultra-orthodox Jews who survived in the large Ghetto until its final destruction. Or, maybe they were among those shot in the streets while I slept in the farmer's barn.

This, I will never know.

I often wonder why I was spared. Why did G-d lead me out of the Ghetto that night? Why was I protected as I ran through the fields, escaped from the labor camp, and survived fighting with the partisans? Why was I kept alive?

Today I believe the answer is simple: I survived so I could tell this story, to bear witness to what I saw. I survived to give testimony that may help others understand how hatred and bigotry can lead to evil and death. I survived to proclaim: "Never again! Never again!"

Eleven million people were murdered in the Holocaust. Six million were Jews, half of whom came from Poland. The other five million were non-Jews, murdered for their religious or political beliefs, for their lifestyle choices or their nationality. Bigotry, racism, and hatred were the root of this horrific crime against humanity, and as long as intolerance exists in the world, it can happen again. I spend a good deal of my time teaching children about the holocaust and sharing my experiences. I do this so they will know what happened. I do this so they will understand the horrible power of hate and bigotry.

Every day, I try to forget what I went through during the war. I try to extinguish the memories of what I saw and experienced. But late at night, when the rest of the world is sleeping, I lie awake, reliving those terrible days. My memories flash like a movie across the ceiling above my bed. I cannot forget what happened to my family. I cannot forget the pain that I experienced.

Although I cannot forget what happened, I try to forget the hate I felt, for hate only makes us bitter and destroys our spirits. I try to live with love and forgiveness in my heart, the way my father and mother taught me to live so many years ago.

I focus on the acts of kindness that saved my life during those terrible years. I remember and am grateful for the times when people risked their lives to save mine, for the kindness, and sometimes even friendship, that gave me the strength and resilience to survive another day.

Most of all, I am thankful to G-d for protecting me. I felt his guidance and care even in my darkest hours. I never lost hope. I never lost faith, for I knew that, even though my family, my friends, and my home were gone, I was never completely alone.

G-d was always at my side.

MENACHEM TAIBLUM

After spending his years as an 11 through 15 year old alternately eluding and fighting the Nazis in Poland, and then spending more than two years after the war unable to leave Europe, Menachem was in among the some of the first groups legally allowed to immigrate into the new state of Israel in 1948.

In Israel, during his time in a "Newcomers" camp, he had the great opportunity to study for a cantorial career with one of the greatest cantors of the 20th century, Moishe Kosowicki. After his time in the IDF, during almost one year of which he served as a driver for the main Rabbi, Major Rabbi Goren he married in 1951 and they had a daughter in 1952. He worked in the desert driving huge Euclid trucks and then worked in the orange orchards.

The Jewish newspaper "New Moment" in San Paulo, Brazil offered him a job. While learning Portuguese he worked on a linotype machine, then spent the rest of his fifteen years in Brazil as a reporter and journalist. He also volunteered as an interpreter for the police.

When he immigrated to the United States in 1972, immigration gave him the middle name, Manny because they couldn't spell Menachem.

His wife and he owned a "bungalow colony" in the Catskill Mountains of N.Y. State, down the road from the famous Grossinger's hotel, where he sometimes served as cantor for their services. In the fall they went to Miami, Florida and ran a small hotel for the winter.

Every place Manny lived he found work as a cantor. His greatest pleasure was in making people happy, laughing and having fun. He worked on the Yiddish stages in Miami, the Catskill Mountains and in California, sharing his jokes and singing in several languages.

Manny has resided in Portland, Oregon for sixteen years, working as a cantor, sharing G-d's gift to him, his beautiful voice, with many worshipers and friends.

CYNDIE MEYER

Cyndie Meyer writes for business and health care in the Pacific Northwest. She is a registered dietitian, a public health professional, and holds a degree in humanities. Meyer was honored to help Mr. Taiblum tell how faith, family, friendship, and the kindness of strangers helped him survive the horrors of the holocaust.

Made in the USA
San Bernardino, CA
22 February 2017